COMING HOME

A MEMOIR

SAWYER COLE HOBSON

PRAISE FOR SAWYER COLE HOBSON

"Sawyer Cole's memoir *Coming Home* is such a heartfelt, personal journey through love and identity and coming-of-age. The vulnerable way they share their life's story could help so many people in claiming their own. I read it with my heart in my throat and am grateful that Cole is here and writing their experience."

Alicia Thompson, National Bestselling Author of *Love in the Time of Serial Killers*

"Brave. beautiful, and raw. Cole leaves their soul right there on the page."

Shannon Jump, Author of *My Only Sunshine*

"Sawyer Cole's heart shines in this honest, raw, hopeful, and beautifully written memoir. ***Coming Home*** is equal parts battle cry and comforting embrace; an account of deep trauma and healing, and a call to action as the queer community continues fighting for basic rights. Cole writes with incredible sensitivity, care, and love that can be felt on every page. Readers, especially those needing to hear "you are enough", welcome home."

Courtney Kae, Author of *In the Event of Love*

"Every so often, a memoir comes along that touches your heart, soul, and funny bone. Sawyer Cole's remarkable

Coming Home asks you to think while also making you feel. Finding beauty in life's lessons can be challenging, but Cole teaches us about the incredible healing power of love. Not to be missed from this author to watch. "

M.A. Wardell, Debut Author of *Teacher of the Year*

To you, dear reader, on your journey home; may you find the peace and comfort to be your authentic self along the way.

To Alisha, my love, here's you a story.

And to the true superheroes of this story: Abilify and Lamictal.

AUTHOR'S NOTE

Dear Reader,

This book was born out of the content warnings from my life. Make no mistake, there are sweet and hilarious moments to be had, but the point of this book is to be a beacon of light to those like me; those who come from small, rural towns where they never quite fit in.

I want you to take care of your own mental well-being. But for me, my history is full of content warnings including: suicide, suicide ideation, homophobia, transphobia, dead naming, adoption, abandonment, and self-harm.

Please protect your own mental health before you continue on with my book. As it has a happy ending, I do understand the fact that some parts may not be for everyone.

With all my love,
　　Sawyer Cole

PREFACE

I'll be honest, I'm scared out of my mind to have this out there. I fear coming off as pretentious. I've always loved to write, although it was either in journal form, or as of more recent years on and off, blog form… Which is to say I've always written privately, or at least in the context that I've shared a space with only what I wanted out there. But here I sit writing what I feel needs saying, rather than what I *want* to say. This is a totally different feeling… to lay myself bare in front of you. This book is one I've poured my heart, soul, sweat and tears into. Oh, the tears. For so long, I tried to write this. For years, I tried to write the wrong thing.

I wrote this because the words felt trapped inside like a ping pong ball bouncing around my organs. It felt like a disease devouring every bit of my soul from the inside out. It was eating me alive. I wrote this to get it out of my body, so I no longer felt sick. I wrote this book to get it out of me so I wouldn't lose myself in the process of recreating and redis-covering myself. I became so tired of hearing the deafening silence of the teardrops scream silently down my face.

There's beauty in the breakdown. I just had to break down first.

And that's the beautiful thing about endings. We get to decide where to start again. In a sense, this is an ending. This is the proper send off to my younger selves. It's a love letter, not only to you, but to my former selves. The ones I've evolved into and out of as I've elevated higher into my own personal being. I know what you're thinking.. selves? Plural? Yes. Selves. As a queer kid, you are forced to be this heterosexual being that isn't you, and when you come out, you finally get that childhood. You get to explore yourself and sexuality that your heteronormative counterparts already did in their adolescence.

You're already behind.

There are so many "selves" that you evolve into and out of as you're growing. For queer kids, sometimes you fall behind, and it's okay that you finally get to discover that at any age—be it your childhood or your 20s, like me, or even later on down the road. There's no time stamp on becoming your authentic self.

It's okay to mourn who you were while realizing who you were wasn't anyone you ever wanted to be in the first place. It's taken me a long time to come to terms with that. I mourn my childhood for not being able to be my authentic self. Sometimes I'm downright angry at the adults in my life who didn't provide me with that type of safe environment. We could talk all day about how times have shifted, but the fundamental truths of love and acceptance should be the pillars in a family—including the extended familial branches on the tree.

Other times, I'm completely gutted and wish for nothing more than a redo. And while that isn't plausible, I know, I do have a chance—every single day—to live my life out loud as exactly who I want to be. That's a privilege that is not lost on me. I get to be white and trans non-binary, with my nails painted black, my hair cut short and my clothing androgynous without the repercussions my Black and BIPOC queer friends may face. That will never, ever be lost on me because I was afforded the skin color of a supremacist system. I only hope that this system be erased, and a new one takes its place that is equitable for every single person.

I hope within these pages you find the strength to be authentically you, too.

I've read a lot of books and drawn inspiration from them. But none will compare to the words I'm writing now because my story is my own. My story is that of redemption, self-discovery, bursting out of those boxes we're all made at a young age to squeeze into. My story is to every queer person in the South who feels unseen. Who's had to shrink themselves to feel accepted. Who still shrinks at the thought of becoming their authentic self. To the person holding this book now who wants to take up more space than they were given - I see you. This is for you, love.

The question I always come back to is this: do I have the right to take up space and write a memoir of my own? I kept coming back to that for years, making excuses every time for why I didn't. What gave me the right to write when there are thousands—millions—of other queer people who have it worse than me? Excuse after excuse hit me like a ton of bricks. I could excuse my way out of that question with my eyes closed, hands behind my back, with a simple eye roll and scroll as I saw indie author after author publish their books. It left me feeling deflated within myself. I sat in self-pity and wallowed in self-doubt. What could I say that others couldn't or hadn't already said?

Finally, it hit me. Years after trying to write the wrong

thing. Years after focusing on the wrong thing. Years of focusing on the wrong people. (We'll get to that later.) Years of drinking, still, trying to numb the pain. Because I wasn't being true to myself. I had to find myself to write about myself, you know? I couldn't write about what I didn't know. Like I said, there's beauty in the breakdown if you just allow yourself to break down.

Let that marinate for a minute.

Truly digest those words. For so long we've all been told to hold it together, toughen up, don't cry about it. But what if, instead, we stop holding it together, feel all there is to feel about it and let the tears wash away what we're feeling? So what if you cry. What's so wrong with that? Absolutely nothing. We have to learn to sit with our pain before we can truly understand what it's trying to teach us. That's the beauty part of the breakdown.

We often want to get to the 'good parts' of our story without healing from the trauma that got us here. We want to fast forward, but life doesn't work that way. I had to learn how to sit with myself, to immerse myself in the messiness before I could *write* about the messiness. I couldn't write about what I hadn't dealt with. I couldn't write about what I hadn't yet come to terms with. And while I'm still navigating that healing journey, one that will continue to evolve as I do, I'm now at a place I can see clearly. I've pulled up a chair and let the messiness teach *me*. I've asked it questions. *What are you trying to teach me? Where did I misstep? Was I the problem? Who am I? What do I believe in?* Those are hard questions to ask. Even harder to truthfully answer yourself. Even harder still, to correct the course, to change the trajectory.

But questions are necessary as part of your journey. Pull up a seat. Lean in. Listen. And when it no longer serves you, remove yourself from the table.

There are parts of this book that I wrote around intentionally. I don't want you to think coming home and sitting with the mess means you automatically fix it—whatever *it* is. Healing isn't linear. Parts of this story still very much hurt me to this day, and maybe they always will. Much like what you're going through, whatever that may be, it may always hurt. We don't grow away from it; we grow with it. We grow through it. It doesn't get erased; we learn to make peace with what we have. We equip ourselves with the proper tools to heal healthily. Those tools came, for me, in the manner of therapy, talking it out with my fiancée and friends, medication, relaxing, taking several breaks and music. Healing for me won't be the same as healing for you, and that's okay. Just remember to create spaces within yourself to heal so you can get through your messiness, healthily.

It's also important to not hand the tools to someone else. You're the sculptor. Only *you* have your vision. Only *you* know the path you want to take. You are the one equipped to build your future however you see it. Handing these tools to someone else oftentimes leads to disaster. Be it parents, siblings, friends, or significant others. Remember, your vision is yours. You can explain it to them, you can share it with them, but don't let them dictate your future. The tools are yours. The future is yours. Your future is your masterpiece, and yours alone. People can share in it, they can be by your side as you achieve it, but remember that at the end of the day, it's still yours.

The question eventually changed for me once I healed enough to see beyond the hurt. Once I sat down, asked the hard questions, learned from them, gathered the tools scattered about, the question finally became: "Why *not* me?" And, my friends, that was the beginning of coming home to myself. That was the final question I couldn't answer. I could make excuses, sure, but I had no definite answer to bring to the table. And this is your time, too. Why *not* you?

I'm here. I'm queer. I have a voice. A voice that needs to be heard. I've often read a famous quote by Ain Eineziz, "You were given this life because you are strong enough to live it." Well, I'm telling you, I've lived it. More importantly, I've grown through it. The question lingered in my mind: *Why not me?*

As Ru Paul says, "If you can't love yourself, how in the hell you gonna love somebody else?" And folx, we listen to Ru Paul in this space.

COMING HOME

I'M COMING to you from a new space. I'm not who I was. Hopefully, by the time this book is finished, I won't even be who I am writing this now. Growth is important. I always strive to be better tomorrow than I was today. (Thanks Sidney Poitier.) Like Matthew McConaughey says, my hero is myself ten years from now—unobtainable, but someone to always aspire to be, paraphrased.

I'm coming from a place of lessons learned and forgiveness for myself time and time again. I'm now coming from a place of newness; a place of comfort and self-love. I have constantly learned how to love and date and spoil myself. It didn't happen overnight. It's been a journey. An evolution. This book is all about coming home. Not in the physical sense, not even in a spiritual sense, but coming home to my soul… to my mental well-being. Coming home to who I was always destined to be. Unpacking the societal definitions of who I was forced to become. Removing those exhausting layers that were given to me without reprieve and permission. As I continue to grow and evolve as a person, I can finally say, without a shadow of a doubt, I'm home. Now I'm just decorating and updating the insides, ya know?

I haven't always been this way. I haven't always been so self-aware. I haven't always been available to myself. I was once notorious for being part of that "yes" mentality to everyone else, excluding myself. I was, once upon a time, the type of person who would shrink myself to fit the ideas others had set before me. I constantly tried to fit into boxes that weren't designed for me to fit into. I craved that social acceptance. I craved love—even if it came at the expense of self-love and -acceptance. I craved belonging, never knowing that I never even belonged to myself.

Needed to be loved by family? Let me shrink myself into the heteronormative gender binary they saw me as. Needed to be loved by friends? Let me be boy crazy and wear makeup and dress a certain way. Needed to be loved by partners? Let me shrink my mental health problems so I don't seem too needy or whiny.

Are all of these toxic behaviors? Absolutely. Are they all extremely unhealthy? Most definitely. But I didn't know that then. I was still coming home, you see. I was still "finding myself." I was still trying to dually exist in two separate worlds—one created *for* me and the one *I* was creating.

It was a task I truly didn't realize was incredibly harmful to my own well-being. This is why it's so important that as adults we create these safe spaces and environments for the younger generations to authentically be themselves without us forcing anything on them, i.e., gender reveals being a big one. This is where the societal constructs begin. This is where we begin to put people in boxes they may not belong in. This is why it's important that we are educated and knowledgeable about things around us, both as a society and culturally.

I never actually knew what "finding myself" meant in my

twenties. I never knew that it would take hours upon hours and flat-out years of being truly alone to know who I was. I thought I'd find it at the bottom of a bottle in a bar surrounded by friends. Those empty bottles only created literal numbness. Those friends? Over a decade later, I talk to maybe two of them. I'm not saying there's anything innately wrong with bar friends, but I wouldn't rely on those people to be around when you decide to leave the bar scene.

In fact, of those two people I talk to, I wouldn't say I could call them if I broke down on the side of the road should I need assistance, and there's absolutely nothing wrong with growing apart from people but let this be a reminder: choose your friends carefully. Some are for a reason, season, or a lifetime. These types of people are, more often than not, seasonal. Don't let them overstay their welcome. Don't let the seasonal people take up a lifetime.

I thought I'd find it settling for what I thought was a life with someone when I knew she wasn't a right fit for me. There was nothing inherently wrong with her. We got along as well as anyone else does in a semi-healthy relationship. I have no ill feelings toward her now, and honestly, I didn't when we split, either. It was the normal end-of-relationship feelings. She just wasn't "the one." She didn't set my soul on fire.

That relationship was comfortable. I owe a great deal to her career wise, don't get me wrong… But every time marriage came up, especially after that five-year mark, I froze internally. We broke up and got back together more times than I care to recount, but after our final break-up, I spent some time alone. Not only mourning the relationship—it still hurt—but I needed to find who I was. I spent so long before her bouncing from one relationship to the next that I had never got to experience myself. I fought so long *within* that relationship for something and I didn't even know what it was. I just thought that was what I was supposed to be doing.

I'm not telling you to leave your life and loved ones behind and become a monk, but I am telling you there's something to being by yourself that no other person and no substance can give you: time.

Time to heal. Time to think.

Come on and do it with me... unclench your jaw, relax your shoulders, and just... breathe deep. Better? That's what I'm talking about. To just *be*. To exist. To not worry about anything other than taking care of your own well-being. Time to enjoy your own company and presence. We get so caught up in the doing, that we forget to exist in a way that is by ourselves. We forget to enjoy our own company. I quickly found out I didn't know who I was by realizing I didn't ever date myself. I realized really quickly I didn't like myself. Not that I was or am a bad person. I, for so long lived for other people, I didn't know how to live *for* myself. Do you?

I didn't fully understand this in my twenties. Like I said, I never knew what "finding myself" meant. I was just along for the ride back then. I've always been a leader in the sense that I'm a loudmouth and have no qualms about speaking up for injustice; in the career sense I was always in leaderships roles because people trusted in me, but I was slow to come into myself and my own thoughts and feelings during that age. It wasn't until I hit that magical 3-0 that I began to truly start questioning what it meant to by myself and what that looked like for me. *Who am I? What do I believe in? Do I even believe in anything? What are my opinions and thoughts on topics?* I didn't know. I knew my stances, but I wasn't as vocal as I could've been. I wasn't proactive. I didn't know where I fit or belonged. That was scary. The realization that I didn't know who I was.

All I knew was that I was part of the LGBTQIA+ community, more than half my family didn't accept me, and I was tired of shrinking to fit into their preconceived ideas of the answers to those aforementioned questions. Their boxes weren't mine to fit into. This much I knew to be true. But it took me a long time to come to terms with it. It took me even longer to speak it into existence.

Coming to terms with all of this, however, was a different story entirely. A story I'm now ready to share with all of you. Not because I have something to prove or gain, but because I've shared spaces with people who have struggled getting home to themselves. Because I'm not meant to stay quiet. I've been given this life to uplift, encourage, and support where I can, however I can. And I know that. I know how difficult it is to be stuck in a body that isn't quite right. I know how it feels to quietly take up spaces when all you want to do is scream, "THIS ISN'T ME!"

My hope with this book, and always when I open my mouth, is that I help at least one person. If I can do that, I will consider this a successful mission. If I can help change minds and create allies to bring more safe spaces for people within the LGBTQIA+ community in the process, fantastic.

But this story is for those that need to feel seen.

To feel heard.

I see you.

I hear you.

You are loved and worthy and deserve to take up space. You deserve to live authentically. You deserve to have people in your corner cheering you on so loudly your eardrums burst.

You deserve to come home.

TRANSFORMATION

Most people think coming out is either being fully accepted or being shunned completely, and while those things do happen, they can also happen simultaneously. Nuanced with societal constructs of gender identity and the sense of self, coming out is anything but easy. The fears surrounding coming out are like waking up every day and looking in the mirror to see the shell of a person staring back at you.

It's like that anti-depressant commercial you see on TV where they hide behind a mask of a fake smile. It's like being trapped in a body you don't belong in, to some. It's playing out each conversation in your mind before it happens and imaging each scenario. It's exhausting. Take living in the South, in a small rural town, with a predominately Republican family and it intensifies significantly.

Living in this environment hasn't been tranquil in the slightest. We'll touch more on that later, though. Couple that with intersectionality, in which I am privileged by the color of my skin, and I couldn't begin to imagine the strains on mental and physical health, or the lack of safety felt. For that, I will always know I am privileged. That will never go unchecked by me.

Coming out is like knowing you're on the verge of being the freest you have ever felt but not taking the step because you can't see in front of you from the heavy fog. For those like me, it's like taking off your glasses and staring at a Christmas tree… It's unfocused, exhilarating, and slightly terrifying that you can't see shit in front of you—but holy wow, does it look beautiful over there. It's like having the words on the tip of your tongue but your mouth is glued shut. Coming out is terrible and intoxicating at the same time. It's having a lump in your throat and not knowing if it's because you need to scream or cry—more often than not, it's both. It's learning about Eleanor Roosevelt or James Baldwin in school, but their homosexuality was left out of the text. It's listening to music that centers on the societal binary and feeling unheard. It's watching a popular television series, where heteronormativity is centralized, and the homosexual character is problematic or killed off, if there even is one at all. It's having all these thoughts and emotions burning within you with no proper vernacular to express them out loud.

When I came out, in 2007, I had just turned twenty. I didn't have this great defining moment of clarity. I didn't have it all figured out. I was still very much figuring myself out in a world before pronouns—besides the societal binary that already existed; in a world where it was still LGBT and the only books in the bookstore filled maybe a shelf and a half and were hidden in the back of the store. It was all nonfiction and there was extraordinarily little to be said in terms of figuring out the whys behind how you felt. I didn't have the vocabulary we have today. I didn't know pronouns were a thing. I had four additional boxes to choose from and that was it. And even those boxes were taboo and left unspoken. Especially trans. I knew next to no one that was LGBT, and especially not trans.

And here I am now, years later, trans non-binary. It was liberating and terrifying and suffocating all at once. I felt trapped in a body I didn't belong in, although I didn't know how to express that at the time and thought I was just *not straight*. I felt trapped in a world that was binarily too small. I didn't have the words to explain it yet. I just knew I wasn't at home in my own body.

At twenty-years-old I knew I wasn't a heterosexual—that much I knew to be true. And it was the beginning of everything, that one singular fact.

It all began when I cut my hair. (Picture it, Sicily…. Just kidding.) Kids, you still with me?

Anyway, I had just graduated college with my Associates of Arts degree. It was the end of summer. I was living with my dad as I had moved into his house during my junior year of high school and stayed through community college. I can close my eyes and I'm there, sitting in his blue checkered recliner in the corner of the living room, kicked back watching TV—more than likely *Top Chef*—while he slept during the day because he worked third shift.

I was watching one particular episode of *Top Chef*, (season two, for inquiring minds) an early episode, where a female contestant got a little drunk and decided to shave her head because she had always wanted to. Fast forward to the ending, and her hair was short and spikey. I fell in love. I mean, I knew at that exact moment that's how I wanted my hair to look. That precise moment. I didn't really know why. I couldn't put it into words. I just knew it was how I wanted it cut. And it was a euphoric feeling, seeing a female with short hair. My hair, for inquiring minds, was a little past my shoulders. So, it was long enough for people who knew me to notice that drastic of a haircut.

"Holy hell," I thought. "They can do that?" It was the feeling that I could truly do anything. I had never seen a female with a shaved head before, not even with short spikey hair. It was a whole new world.

I was still best friends with a guy I met in college. Now, again, this was 2007, so texting was still very much *not* a thing; iPhones hadn't yet taken over. So, we were *actually on the phone*. Imagine the horror! I vaguely remember telling him that's how I wanted my hair cut. I'm not sure if he believed me when I said that, or how much interest there actually was, but he nonchalantly told me to do it.

That was all the reassurance I needed.

Since I had one person's bout of confidence, I decided then and there that I wanted it chopped off. So, the next day I went to a barber I had grown up around and had it cut off without thinking twice. Hindsight is 20/20, and maybe this should've been the defining moment of my coming out story, but alas, I had no idea of anything—except that I wanted my hair chopped off. This was just a silent step into the journey I was about to finally embark on. And oh, what a sweet journey it has turned out to be.

The way I felt sitting in that chair was out of this world. It was indescribable. I come from a family of hairdressers, so he knew my family. I'm pretty sure he asked if I was sure, then kind of smiled and shrugged and said, "Okay." The memory of the conversation is hazy to me. But I do remember watching my hair fall to the floor, hearing the faint buzz of the clippers on my head and knew my life was beginning… I just didn't know in what context.

I didn't know that in two short months I would change the course of my life for the better. I was unaware that I would finally live. I was highly unaware of how my life would shape-shift into this beautiful, messy, chaotic, and intoxicating *thing* I have come to know as the intrinsically beautiful life I call home.

COMING OUT, PART I

I CAN'T PINPOINT the exact day I came out.

I know it was in September. I know it was roughly a week before our local fair, so probably toward the middle of the month. I know I wasn't intending to come out. I was outed—in a sense—by a family member. I can close my eyes and be transported back in time to that day. Sitting on the floor of my cousin's house in the back bedroom that was turned into a makeshift office because she was in school. It was scary. It was freeing.

It was terrifyingly perfect.

It was during the MySpace days. You know, moody backgrounds and angsty music and *My Top 8* like your entire life revolved around ensuring your friends were distinctively known first. I'm probably showing my age here…

Bueller? Just me?

I digress.

You see, I close my eyes and I see MySpace open on my cousin's laptop. Although, at the time, I had no clue it was *my* page that was open. I should've known, though. No doubt by the blaring of Evanescence or Corey Smith.

I was sitting on the floor, my back against the door, the hallway to my right, adjacent to my cousin's computer desk where she sat, cluttered with books and toys from two of her now three young boys. I see her sitting there thinking she had a MySpace message, when in fact, *I* was the one that had the message. She absentmindedly opened the message, as we talked about god knows what, and watch her face go blank. "Oh, my god," I hear...

And the rest of the world goes quietly numb.

That's when I knew it wasn't *her* MySpace page she was checking.

"What's this?" she asked. A few seconds that felt like years went by as I watched her face go from cheerful to expressionless. "You're gay?"

Fuck.

That was *my* message.

And this is where my coming out story begins.

COMING OUT, PART II

I STARED BLANKLY as she got up and paced the length of the hallway. And the hallway really wasn't that long, but that walk of hers felt like a decade. I watched—as if in slow motion—as she walked away from me.

But it wasn't just *her* that walked away; it was her acceptance of me. The love. The quiet betrayal, even if she didn't mean it, that's what it felt like. She was freaking out; her childhood best friend had recently come out to her as well.

I know we're from a small town where the gay population at that point in time—at least, in my mind—was one: me. So, for her, this information was foreign and unheard of. I can't pinpoint the exact words she said, but it was along the lines of, "Why is this happening to me?"

They were self-centered and not about me or my feelings in any way. Mine were never taken into consideration that day—except for with my dad, but we'll get to that later, and even then, I didn't get to express how I truly felt.

No one asked.

Not my cousin who read my private MySpace message, or my family or friends that I told later that day. I was shaken and wondered what to do next. Obviously, I knew I had to come out; I had no choice. The knowledge that even one single person in the family knew my deepest secret was enough to make me feel like the entire family knew. They were going to in a matter of days, anyway; it was the latest "gossip" after all.

So, I had no choice but to come out right then and there. I was unprepared. I didn't have anything ready to say. I was too lost trying to figure out *my* feelings and grappling with *my* own emotions to even consider telling my family. Yet there I still sat with my innermost feelings exposed like I was sitting there naked on display for the world to see.

I'd like to stop for a moment and point out that just because one person may know you're out doesn't necessarily mean you *have* to come out to the entire world in thirty-six hours like I did. But I knew my family, and I knew the consequences of one person knowing.

Each story will be different, and by no means am I saying to do what I did. This was my choice, and at the time, it felt like my only way out because I had no one to talk to about it. Instead of freezing, I came out with it like word vomit before I could even process the events or the mechanics of what I was actually doing.

I had no books to help me.

No peers to guide me.

No mentors to bounce ideas off.

I was virtually alone, and this was the best-case scenario for me rather than tucking my tail and running. I was out, and that was how it was going to be in my mind.

The overall memory is hazy to me. I know a lot of things, but pieces of the conversations and day are lost to me. One male cousin was excited we could go to the mall and "scope out girls" together. One of my aunts, who now condemns my "behavior", said she didn't doubt it because "I came out like a football player at birth."

Whatever that means.

I've never understood the correlations of sports to male figures as if women and nonbinary/gender non-conforming people cannot be athletic. But again, those small-town vibes are real.

I left in a hurry because I felt claustrophobic. I remember being on the phone with various cousins, maybe one was face-to-face, I don't remember who in the family I told versus who came to know by word of mouth. (News travels quickly in this family. Especially if it's *drama*.)

But suddenly, my small-town felt like a crackerjack box and I was *Clifford the Big Red Dog*. I had outgrown my town in a matter of minutes. I had outgrown everything I knew because of a singular MySpace message read at the wrong time, by the wrong person.

There's something so cathartic yet frightening about having your deepest secret exposed. Dear reader, don't get me wrong: I was angry, and scared, but I was finally free.

And I still had to tell my dad.

The hardest call to make was to him. Not because I thought he would be disappointed. It was the opposite, actually. I knew he would love me just the same as he did the minute before I told him. See, my dad adopted me when I was six years old. He's been in my life since I was one. This man's love for me is the purest form of unconditional love there is, and I'm not sure why I was so afraid of telling him. He's the life of the party. He's funny, charismatic and can make even the most stoic person laugh until they piss themselves without even trying. Most of my favorite childhood memories are because of him. He's the best, and I'd put him up against anyone. But I was afraid of how he might react. When, in reality, his words that day are the only ones I remember clearly.

I was driving down my high school road, Falcon Road, right before I got to the last curve coming up to the stop sign, when he picked up the phone. I told him I had something to tell him, and it felt like I was driving fast but sitting still. His initial reaction was to ask if I was pregnant. I assured him I most certainly was not. (The irony, am I right?)

When I told him I liked girls, I began to cry out of sheer exhaustion, fear, and the overall feeling of not being able to take the words and insert them back in my mouth. "Oh," he said, "Well." A slight pause as he takes it all in. "Do you feel like the weight has been lifted off your shoulders now?" I replied, "Yes," and he told me he loved me and then proceeded to ask if I was coming home that night.

That was the best conversation we've ever shared to date. I know it wasn't this over-sharing of emotions. It wasn't this *gigantic* moment. But the smaller moments seem to hold the most space. We don't do that in my family, anyway, the sharing of all these emotions. (Unless it's anger. We do *that* well.) Not because we don't love one another, we just don't share emotions well. Call it generational trauma.

But the amount of room he gave me to be myself when I needed it most was unparalleled. He allowed me space to be me. I didn't know it was at the time. But through coming out as nonbinary and a legal name change fourteen later, that's exactly what he did that day in September. He gave me permission to be exactly who I was. And that, my friends, was what I needed, and what I wish for every one of you.

I can't say the same about the rest of the conversations I had on the topic.

And like I said earlier, I don't remember every conversation as clearly as the one I had with my dad. I remember fragments. For instance, I was on the road, at a stoplight at this old gas station—right by Shelbie and Mo's (we'll get to them later, remember their names, they're significant)—when I told my sister.

Now, she's the type that likes to ask questions. To process. Ask more questions. Process a little more. And not say a whole lot in between. This was, of course, nerve-racking for me. I needed reassurance from any and everyone. I needed *something* to hold onto. I understand now that that's just how some people are. It wasn't that she was upset or anything, she was processing a newer version of her sibling. And that's a lot to digest for a seventeen-year-old.

I know what you're thinking: she didn't offer support. She didn't celebrate you first thing. But let me stop you there. Sure, kids and teens nowadays are equipped with the vocabulary and super open to sexuality, but remember, I come from a small town and back then, we didn't have LGBTQIA+ representation like we do now.

We barely had Ellen.

That was the extent.

And even then, her sexuality wasn't spoken about either. This was huge for my sister. And I can't take that away from her experience. It was all new. We simply didn't know any queer people.

Not. A. Single. One.

I'm not negating the fact that I felt desperately alone. I wish my sister had been supportive during that initial conversation. Or spoken up and said she loved me or shared *some* words of encouragement. We all deserve that. We all deserve to feel loved every second we are alive. What I am saying is that people also deserve to process their own emotions while still being supportive. We can properly navigate those two while being loving and supportive, without hurting one another in the process.

On the flip side, my mom and I didn't particularly see eye-to-eye then; we were on one of our infamous "outs," so my sister, after still not being able to process what I had just told her, was the one to relay the news to our mom.

I have no idea how that conversation went.

I know Mom was upset. I know she drove to Memaw's, who is a devout Christian, actually an ordained minister, so they probably prayed about it, I'm not sure. I wasn't privy to how that conversation went, either. I remember driving by Memaw's house a few times and seeing Mom's blue Honda CRV there, wanting to feel close but not wanting to stop for fear of the abandonment I was already feeling. They were sitting outside on the front porch, no doubt freaking out in their own ways. The conversation taking place between them would've hurt me to my core had I been there. So, I never could muster up the courage to stop.

It was better that way; I just kept driving.

I've never felt as alone as I did on that drive. I cried. I can't remember where I drove. I just kept crying and I kept driving. I felt relief and paralyzing fear of what was to come next: telling my friends and my church. And if any of you have ever been to church in the South... Well, welcome to the third portal to hell.

I sat cross-legged on my bed at my dad's that night while he was at work. I called Alan, the friend that gave the go ahead on my hair cut, and of whom, I should mention, actively said he was a Democrat and believed everyone deserved equality (oddly enough, that didn't apply here.) He actually got me to register Independent rather than Republican like my family. So, thanks for that, pal.

Anyway, I called Alan first, figuring I would have a solid ally. I didn't even know what that word meant yet, I just knew I needed *someone* in my corner that day. I could not have been further from the truth. As I've said previously, I don't remember the exact verbiage, but he played me the song, "Who Knew" by P!nk, and the conversation was very reminiscent of the one I had with the cousin who accidently outed me. He made it all about him. I wasn't completely sure how *my* sexuality effected *him*, but his feelings somehow took precedence over mine, and that never sat right with me. (Can we just stop for a minute and recognize the irony of him playing me a P!nk song while she's such a staunch advocate for LGBTQIA+ rights?)

Anyway, that abruptly ended my friendship with Alan. To this day, fourteen years later, I've only spoken to him a handful of times through social media messages. (Don't worry, I detoxed and removed him completely for my own mental health a few years ago.) But the point remains, I lost a friend who I thought would be there for me. I cried yet again. So far, my day was anything but happy, except for the gleaming redemption that was my dad. And even then, at the time, it was anticlimactic, and I had yet to hear any affirming words of support.

I should pause to mention that despite this, I knew I was loved. But it was the first time I questioned the depth of that love, and that's a weird place to be.

It's lonely.

It's the knowledge that family and friends surround you, people who are supposed to love you unconditionally, and then finding out (very quickly) that their love is conditional.

Their love is based on their own ideals, their expectations of who you're supposed to be.

It's being alone in a crowded room.

It's learning to breathe differently.

It's learning about yourself, by yourself.

It's entering this new world and knowing no one.

It's euphoric and at the same time, frightening.

It's being born in a new light but having no one to share it with.

CHURCH

WHAT LAY AHEAD NEXT WAS church. I knew this part was going to be the hardest, so I waited until Wednesday night, which, by deduction, meant I came out on a Tuesday, for church. We were having AWANA's (Approved Workmen Are Not Ashamed, named after a bible verse) night, a Southern Baptist affiliate program for kids, and I was a teacher.

I met the director in the parking lot, tears already streaming down my face as soon as I got out of the car.

"Susan," I said. "You aren't going to let me come back to church." She looked at me with bewilderment. "I'm gay. You aren't going to let me come back and teach anymore."

I don't remember her reply. She was shocked, though. Stunned to silence.

I don't remember anything from that night other than somehow being escorted inside to *talk* and being cornered by three other women of whom I thought were my confidants.

My mentors and friends. One cornering me alone in a room in the back of the church telling me I *never accepted jesus into my heart* and I was never really a christian. That one singular moment still sits with me. We sat close together on a couch, facing one another, and she looked me dead in the eyes and spoke those words to me.

I was an adult by definition, but I have never in my life felt so small. Even now, I can't come up with a moment where I have felt that way since. When I think of moments that hurt the most, those words, at that time, cut the deepest. Those words came crashing down on me like tidal waves. I would never reconcile with the church again.

And I haven't.

I remember another time, later that week, hell, maybe that same night, being cornered again by now four women saying the same things, but this time it was in the basement of one of their homes.

Praying the gay away.

I can't remember how I left. Or why I had agreed to meet them or go with them in the first place, really. I just remember trying to grasp at straws for these people who I grew up with, who I babysat for, who I shared family meals with and sleepovers, and secrets… people I wanted to still love me. I was very much a young adult wanting to find my way in life, and these people were supposed to be the ones who loved and accepted me. I couldn't have been further from the truth that Wednesday night.

I was wrong.

There's truly no hate like Christian love.

And that night I felt every ounce of it.

I felt the stares. I felt the recoil of touch. How I was still longing for someone to just tell me I was okay and loved. I was with people who should've been that comfort, that steadiness, instead, I was with people who withdrew, guarded themselves, like they had never known me before; like I was a leprous stranger. Oh, how the tables had turned within twenty-four hours.

I grew up with a saying that, "Church hurt is the worst type of hurt." I spent years in a cross-shaped shadow I could never escape from. What kind of life is that? With the shadows looming down on me like the Mothman prophecies. I never knew what that meant until I came out. And now I know. Now I know that it isn't just hurt from a friend. Or a failed relationship. Or a fight with a loved one. It's much deeper than that.

You spend time with these people. You pour your heart out to them. You're at your most vulnerable at times. Sometimes laying out vulnerabilities, i.e., coming out, of which you know will change the outcomes of the relationships, but when you expect to see compassion, or grace, or love, that's usually when you don't get it.

They recoil and strike venomously.

That's what happened in my situation. And it's echoed a lot throughout churches with LGBTQIA+ people as well. I came out at church. And I was received with anything but love, compassion, grace.

I was shunned.

Dare I say hated. Removed in an instant; cast aside from those who were supposed to take me in. I became leprous. An outcast. And rather than loving the outcast, I was thrown away.

This happens every single day in the South. In a place where you're supposed to be accepted—not in spite of, but because of.

Where love is the foundation of their faith.

What a fucking sham.

I grew up in churches ranging from Pentecostal with my Memaw, to non-denominational, to Southern Baptist to Evangelical; you name it, I guarantee I was there. Sometimes twice on Sunday and again on Wednesday. Especially in my teenage years. You could find me there every time the doors were open. Which, come to find out, is a lot when you live in the South. It consumed all of my free time and then some.

In my younger days, I was there with patent leather shoes, frilly dresses, white socks with lace at the top and my hair teased to jesus on Sunday morning. You know what Dolly says, "The higher the hair, the closer to god." Except I hated every second of it, and I'm sure god was nowhere to be found in those Southern backwoods' churches. Not because it was one denomination over another, but because I don't think a spiritual deity showed up in the same place where people hated one another. But this wasn't a lesson I wouldn't learn until much later.

Don't get me wrong, there was a time in my life when I was right beside the people in those buildings every chance I got. I played drums for the church band, I was a youth leader, I helped run the sound board, and taught AWANA's—a Southern Baptist child and teens approach to teaching the bible to underage youth. Y'all, I was in the thick of it for a long time during my teen years—mostly all of them.

There's nothing wrong with that, I want to be clear, but when it becomes people mandating your spirituality or your relationship with your chosen Creator, it becomes dangerously close to, if not totally, brain washing and fake. And that's where I was.

I was at the cusp of a cult.

I was in the thick of people pleasing and doing what was expected of me, when in reality, it shouldn't have been about the people at all.

I quickly learned that lesson. I learned that it was all about the people. I learned what it meant to truly be hurt. I spent most of my life trying to survive this type of hurt, and it came full circle. I spent most of my life trying to figure out how to live up to the impossible standards these people set before me. A daunting task, no doubt.

And I have since spent my life trying to correct the course.

My mom and I butted heads a lot as I was growing up. I wasn't an easy child, I know this. There were problems that could've been resolved had the adults been adultier, but I was also packed with (ignored) mental health issues as well. So, to say that I wasn't an easy child, was to say I had unresolved mental health issues and issues the adults could have answered to but didn't. It was the 90s after all; mental health wasn't really a priority weighing on anyone's conscience, especially within kids.

I acted out.

Not through alcohol or drugs or sexual promiscuity, but more along the lines of attitude. I was packed with it. I would, as the old saying goes, argue with a brick wall—and win.

Anyway, to alleviate some of the stressors from both my mom and me, one of my aunts gave me an ultimatum one year. I was like twelve, maybe thirteen. I could stay there with my mom, or go to church camp with her, where I'd be away from Mom for a whole week.

SOLD.

Off to camp I went, and the course of my teenage years because angsty christian music with a side of naivety. Oh, the glory days. *Cringe.*

Looking back, those days are bizarre to me. It was like I was a different person. I can see myself trying so hard to fit in and be accepted. It makes me mourn myself all over again for trying to fit into those perfectly shaped boxes. It makes me realize I was trying so hard to be who everyone wanted me to be. I was trying too hard to be liked and included.

It breaks my heart that teenage me didn't know who they were and was looking in every wrong box trying to find themself.

Adolescence is such an angsty time, filled with so much emotion, to add in a cult-like brainwashing is something else entirely. Don't get me wrong, there's a line between spirituality and religion. I believe people can be spiritual, to believe in their chosen faith, but also not become a religious nut—I was brought up and continued to be for the majority of my teen years—a religious nut.

It became what I ate, slept, breathed. There was no distinct separation between my identity and my faith. The two merged and it's both cringy and scary to view now, but that's the reality of what it was for me back then. I just wanted to be accepted and loved, and I fought like hell to make sure I was included in a space somewhere.

That was *my* space.

And I did everything I could to maintain my position there. I became so active in church I was there every time the church doors were open. If I wasn't in school, playing drums in the marching band, or coaching sports, I was either at the church or with people from the church doing churchy things.

I was sucked in.

All because I wanted to belong somewhere. It was about the people rather than the spiritual. And that, my friends, is what most churches are like down South: a popularity contest. We've all seen them; the money, the high-tech churches. It's just too peopley, ya know?

I'm not saying all churches are bad. I know there are churches that are accepting and loving and even have LGBTQIA+ members and pastors, however, the ones I was brought up in, weren't it. They were not the slightest bit inclusive. They definitely weren't welcoming. And so, this is my experience.

I would hate to take away someone's personal faith or belief based on my experience. But this was fourteen years ago. We've come a long way since that time of acceptance. Especially in the South where this is still happening behind closed doors. Where, in a state where it's still legal to hold conversion therapy, it's perfectly acceptable to ostracize someone for their sexual orientation, gender identity, et al. In a state that held the dreaded bathroom bill.

Welcome to North Carolina: home of closed-mindedness.

Welcome to a state where it's still legal to marry your cousin, but you're outcasted for being gay.

#Murica.

FINDING MY VOICE

It's been a wild ride discovering who I am. There's an anonymous quote that says, "Every next level will demand another you." And I am 100% here to tell you, I was exactly who I needed to be at every point in time throughout life.

I needed to be carefree with reckless abandon in my early twenties.

I needed to mature and grow up, but still not have my shit together in my mid-late twenties. Now I'm not telling you to wile out and forfeit everything you've worked for. What I am telling you is that I had to grow up and have fun along the way, and I did.

I had so much fun.

I made mistakes.

I was an amazing friend.

I was even a terrible friend.

But I had fun. I grew up. I learned.

And I partied. And when I say I partied, I mean, I'm laughing at the fact myself and friends pitched tents in the back of one of their yards, drank moonshine from water bottles (was it home-made and extremely illegal? Snitches get stitches.) and thought we were living our best lives. And to be honest, we were. We were at the level we were supposed to be at. Rowdy, raucous and rambunctious early twenty-year-old's just living life to the fullest. Let me tell you, fun was had. Nights were blacked out.

Actually, and this is embarrassing (I think I've told maybe a handful of people, and we'll blame a total sense of being depressed mixed with alcohol and new environments), but I was so drunk one night at a bar. It was this local country joint. A *country* bar. And listen, if any of you have ever lived in the South, you know a country bar, and its people, do not typically mix well with queer people who look like me: trans-nonbinary and androgynous. And I was what we call a "baby gay" so I was probably rainbowed out. If you know, you know. Phew.

A "baby gay" for those of you who may not know, is someone who recently came out. Baby gays are new to the LGBTQIA+ community and are usually adorned in rainbow paraphernalia from head to toe. It's a clear indicator of who the baby gays are. And this isn't a derogatory term or phrase. Rather, it's endearing. It's a rite of passage. We all go through it; where we're so proud of who we are, and we want the world to know. It's a special moment in life that can only truly be appreciated by being *in* it. You can't explain it; it just is.

But anyway, there I was, at this country bar, because I was young and didn't know any better, with a group of my friends. I was underage, which translates to: I drank my vodka straight from the bottle (we call this pregaming) at the house while we were getting bar ready. And this wasn't top shelf vodka by any means. This was straight up bottom shelf, Burnett's Vodka. Shit was nasty. But I was twenty and didn't know any better. I turned that bottle up and got shit-faced. When you know better, you do better, friends.

I did not know better.

Nonetheless, I was turned up on this nasty ass bottom of the bottom shelf vodka, and obviously, I had to "break the seal," you know? So, my drunk ass goes to the restroom. Let me lay the scene for you: this hallway is *covered* with mirrors. Lined on both sides. Like four feet deep, top to bottom, in mirrors. Now picture it, friends, a drunk person staggering down a hallway lined with mirrors on either side, dare I say, *bouncing* side to side. See any problems?

Let me make it even more clear for those of you that's never been drunk in a hallway full of mirrors: I bounced so much between these mirrors, I thought I was bumping into people, and I had the drunken audacity to say, "Excuse me" every. single. time. This made for a long night.

Imagine trying to find the way to the toilet while bumping into yourself, saying excuse me to your doppelgänger, in a bathroom full of probably less drunk, older, heterosexual adults. Fun times were had. That night? Probably wasn't fun at the time but the story makes for a good time now.

Now, I know you're wondering what in the hell this has to do with finding your voice being piss drunk in a country bar in the South as a queer person but let me explain.

When you're *not* piss drunk in a country bar as a queer person, you're a sober queer in a country bar, and both are problematic when you look like a prepubescent little boy trying to waltz your way into the women's restroom. You get manhandled. Literally. By grown ass men. Grabbing your arm, jerking you backwards, while you weigh in at a buck twenty, oblivious to the world around you.

That shit *changes* you.

To be walking to the restroom, minding your own business, when all of a sudden, an arm grabs you and sends you catapulting backwards nearly knocking you off your feet while you're being yelled at that you're going to the wrong bathroom and obscene words are being spewed in your direction. It doesn't help cowboy Chad is already piss drunk himself. The first half a dozen times this happened shook me to my core.

Yeah, I said half a dozen.

Yeah, it's happened more times than I care to recount, but let's say it's more than a dozen in the span of fourteen years.

It was easier to handle while drunk. It didn't seep into your mind. It didn't linger. You just needed to piss. You weren't analyzing the fact you were getting assaulted publicly and no one was coming to your defense. You weren't calculating who was escorting you to the restroom. You weren't thinking about all the men surrounding you that were two times your size and ready to pounce. You weren't preparing for the verbal assaults that were going to come your way. It was easier when you were drunk.

You just didn't think.

But sober, though? Sober, your mind took over. You calculated everything. Sober you was petrified and refused to use any public restrooms and fitting rooms. Why? Because you were accosted at such a young age for trying to use the restroom. You were assaulted, beat up, verbally attacked. You wore bruises because you were just trying to piss.

Sober you knew better than to go into uncharted territory. And that is why today, you'll never see me use a public restroom or fitting room. Fourteen years later. Some things may have changed for the better, but you can't fix ignorance.

And society is very much, still ignorant.

Experiences change you. They shape you. They swallow

you up whole and spit you out into bits and pieces. What happens after that is up to you.

This is how I found my voice.

By sitting with experiences such as this. By collecting those bits and pieces and putting myself back together. A little tattered, a little torn, but the last time I checked, broken crayons still color.

I could tell you a dozen more instances where I've been accosted, followed into the restroom, been verbally attacked, but you get the idea. Sitting with these experiences and situations—like the aforementioned—makes you do a lot of reflecting. Sitting with them means sitting with the fear, with the sadness, with the grief and heartache. Getting up from the table after you've heard what they have to say, you come up with a new sense of belonging to yourself.

You leave the table with a new pride.

You stand up for yourself.

You may be more guarded in some respects, but you also know who you are.

COMING OUT (AGAIN)

I'VE COME OUT, it feels, like half a dozen times. I came out as a lesbian at twenty-years-old. Again, as non-binary at thirty-three. A name change at thirty-four. Out again as trans-nonbinary at thirty-four. Coming home to yourself is constantly coming out if you're anything but cisgender and heterosexual. It's this irrational fear of not being accepted for who you are. It's this irrational fear of not being loved for who you are. It's a fear of abandonment at every coming out. It's wondering if this is the last straw for your family to give up on you and say, "ENOUGH!"

Coming home to yourself is exhausting when you aren't cis het. It's a lot of personal work. Development. Trying it on. Testing the waters. It's an ebb and flow. It's also stressful.

Talk about feeling stressed out—it's a constant struggle to feel at peace. It's not knowing if you're truly at peace with yourself or if you're just living to make sure you don't cause any more confusion to those around you. It's trying to live authentically but not having the correct vernacular to make it that way. It's growing up as the language evolves, too.

I didn't have the language we do now, back then. I didn't

have the vernacular to express how I felt or who I was. It's not wanting to make those around you uncomfortable. For those that have kids, we talk so much about needing a village to raise them, but we fail to forget that adults need villages, too. We need to surround ourselves with people who want to see us thrive, not make us uncomfortable. That's sometimes the hardest part about coming out; not knowing who stays in your village and who leaves—be it willingly or unwillingly.

It's educating yourself about yourself.

It's endless hours of researching.

I didn't simply wake up and decide, "Hey, I'm trans non-binary." I spent hours upon hours researching everything I could find. *Does this fit me? How about this? What about this?* It's asking yourself what fits you, and to do this, you have to be in touch with yourself. You have to know who you are to an extent. Asking questions about yourself, to yourself, is such an integral part of coming home. It's a realization that you matter enough to figure out yourself.

I came out as non-binary after hours and days of research, again, realizing that something was off after about a year. Something was missing. I didn't feel like I was at home within myself. I still didn't feel *right*.

So, I did what anyone does when they feel the same way: I researched. *Again*. It was exhausting. I researched everything from non-binary to transgender to both. I looked up every single term to see if it fit me. (Human Rights Campaign has a solid dictionary for terms if you need a resource. It's an excellent one.)

This is an incredibly important part of coming out. Search engines are our best friends. Some of us just know we're part of the community. But that doesn't change the fact that hours go into wondering what makes us different; what makes us unlike those around us.

Questioning our existence.

What sets us apart.

If you've never had the luxury of never questioning yourself, your sexuality or cringed at your birth name, you don't understand the extent to which we feel less than our cis het counterparts. You don't understand how hearing our deadname (the name given to us at birth, of which we no longer use) causes physical pains. You don't understand not feeling at home in your own body. You don't understand your skin crawling when you see yourself naked in the mirror, not liking the image staring back at you.

Googling your identity is humbling. For me, it felt like I was destined to be an outcast forever because I could not for the life of me figure out why I felt so far detached from myself. I still didn't know the term gender dysphoria, so I was at a loss. I didn't understand that even coming out as non-binary hadn't changed anything.

A piece was still missing.

It was only when I was doing a paper for my undergraduate program that I decided to use the college search engine to up the ante on my quest for normalcy. I was writing a paper on a queer topic, I can't recall it now, it was irrelevant to my own personal inquiries, but it did get me questioning my gender even more so.

I had never heard of anyone else being 'trans non-binary' so I thought I was the only one. Turns out, I'm not. It's totally a thing! I didn't feel so alone once I found others who were part of this community, too. I felt validated and true in my own way. It's amazing what can happen when you realize you aren't the only one.

It's liberating.

It's freeing.

Knowing that you are justified in your way of existing.

You matter.
You're important, yes.
But you aren't alone.
And that's the most important thing.

Coming out again and again and again (and even again), is something straight people take for granted that they don't have to endure. We have to come out at every new job. At the TSA line wanting a specified gender to pat us down. During school when we are deadnamed during roll call. Not to mention, meeting new people, using public restrooms or fitting rooms, meeting someone's family—it's always the fear of having to come out all over again. Like, "Yeah, hi, I'm Sawyer Cole, and I'm trans non-binary. My pronouns are they/them. Can you please stop trying to figure me out?"

It's annoying and stressful and you never know how people are going to take it, much less, you. People need signs on their head that say, "I am a safe space." Otherwise, things just get complicated. More complicated than they need to be.

Coming out over and over and over again is annoying, depressing at times, and overall, disheartening. It feels as if no one truly understands you. Imagine, friends, you having to announce your sexuality every time you entered somewhere new to the strangers around you and waiting to see if you were going to be accepted or not. Imagine having to be fearful of walking into a room. (Let's also not forget intersectionality that comes into play here, too.) For me, it makes me not want to go anywhere new, especially in the South.

DEAR OWEN CONLEY

THERE'S no easy way to write this chapter. There's no easy way to sit with the grief that is yourself as you reckon with the ghosts that still haunt you. There's no way to stop and smell the roses when the roses are dead to you, but I hope you'll sit with me as I navigate with you the fear of living by the fear of dying.

There's just no way but through.

And we'll walk together through this, through the lens of a queer person living in the South. Not wanting to die, but not wanting to live like this either.

Just wanting to feel like a valuable person in society.

Just wanting to feel like a person.

Just wanting to *feel*.

And it all to be accepted.

As I write this, The Don't Say Gay bill in Florida just passed the House, waiting on the Senate's verdict. As I write this, Texas is doubling down on harming the trans, non-binary and gender non-conforming youth. As I write this, there are thirty-four states that are seeking anti-trans bills all over the country, and that number will no doubt change by publication date. And we wonder why LGBTQIA+ youth are at risk for suicide, depression and bullying in comparison to their cisgender, heterosexual counterparts.

To preface this chapter, let me tell you that I've lost a cousin to suicide. I've just recently lost one of my "kids," trans, from an old job as recently as this year, at the young age of twenty-three. This chapter hits close to home not only with my own personal emotions, but because I've been directly impacted by loss from suicide.

I've felt the shockwaves of grief coming at me like a tsunami. The ghosts of them keeping me awake. Not because I think they're selfish. Suicide is *never* selfish. It's the final act of depression. It's the final act of emotions too big for a body that isn't well-equipped. It's the final act of too many feelings for a bodily system that isn't built for the impact.

Before I get to that, I'll begin with my story. I was around twelve years old, and I'm not sure where I learned it exactly. There weren't shows like *13 Reasons Why* on TV back in the 90s. We didn't discuss self-harm or suicide. But I knew I had pain inside me that needed an outlet. I was buried under the weight of struggling to survive and had no way to get it out.

I was feeling emotions bigger than myself as a kid, and I had no healthy means of speaking them into existence. It's the feeling of being lost in your own body. It's being lost in lone-liness and having no clear path back to yourself. It's feeling like there's an ocean in your soul and you're drowning.

It's not knowing what comes next.

It's not knowing how to breathe, or if you even want to.

I started self-harming with I was twelve-years-old. I won't give details because I don't believe in giving access to people on the cusp of self-harm the means to do so, but that's when I started. I don't remember the time; I don't remember how I knew what to do.

I just remember the feeling.

The feeling of release.

I remember feeling like I was finally in control of how I felt. I was in control of *something*. For the first time, I felt like I had it all figured out; only I didn't. I was just caught up in feelings. I was caught up in an illusion of safety. I was harming myself and that wasn't okay. *I* wasn't okay. I spent most of my life just learning to survive. I wasn't equipped with the tools to thrive.

My best friend saw the places on my arm and immediately inquired about what they were. For this, I wasn't as grateful then as I am now. She sought out an adult, as she should have. I was taken to the counselor's office immediately once they found out what was going on.

Her office was in the middle of the eighth grade hallway, first door to the right. It was one of those long hallways that seemed never-ending. There was a couch in there. I don't remember much else about that room. It looked comfortable, like someone lived there. It felt like what a home would feel like—well-loved.

She offered me herbal tea. To my knowledge, that was the first time I had ever had tea. I wasn't left alone for the remainder of the day. The counselor called my mom, but I don't remember much else. I don't remember meeting with the counselor or my mom; I don't even remember her name or what she looked like. I don't remember anything but knowing I had to go to therapy outside of school. It was scary and I felt like I had done something wrong, and all these adults were suddenly paying attention me.

Walking into the big gymnasium during some sport or another and my team sitting against the bleachers as our coach talked about how I never gave up—how I persevered and continued on in spite of not making any sports the year prior and working hard to come back and make the teams the following year—I felt like an imposter. I felt like all eyes were on me and they knew my secret, that I was just faking it. I felt scared. I felt like I was alone. It was actually the most alone I had ever felt even though the coach was praising me.

I began counseling, despite it being short-lived, the following week, I believe. I took anger management. Answered question after question. It was here I was first diagnosed with clinical depression. At the age of twelve.

I fought adamantly against taking medicine—and won. I was too much for my mom to handle, so she gave in. I'm sure she didn't want me taking medicine at that age either. What I would give to go back and agree to medication. What a difference that would've made for my mental well-being. Sadly, that wasn't the case. I don't remember visiting this counselor or having sessions like I was supposed to. I believe it ended after the medicine altercation.

I kept self-harming.

Fast-forward to age fourteen. I was sitting at my older cousin's house with her then husband. A revolver on the coffee table. Their newborn sleeping peacefully in his crib. My cousin and her husband asleep in their room down the hall.

I don't know what possessed me to pick it up.

It was loaded.

I had no experience with weapons. But it was there, before I knew it: in my hands. The cool metal in my palm. The taste of the short barrel was in my mouth before I could register the full grasp of what was happening.

I just wanted the pain to stop.

I wanted my insides to stop screaming. I wanted my brain to be quiet. I wanted to feel alive. And that was the only way I knew how to feel alive: to silence everything.

My baby cousin started crying in his crib and snapped me back to reality. The reality I was living in. I put down the revolver and picked up a life instead. It took years to understand what that sentence truly meant to me. He went back to sleep, and so did I.

Unscathed, only barely.

I could preach to you gun violence, laws and the rest, but I'll save that for the experts. I will say I should've never had access to that weapon in the first place. What a different ending I could've had. What a different ending so many LGBTQIA+ youth could've had. What a different ending for so many people whose lives were intertwined with those they lost to suicide. I didn't become a statistic, but I can close my eyes and I'm back in that room, tasting the metal in my mouth on that dark and lonely night. How many of us have been there before? Just wanting the pain to pass? Just wanting to feel alive by trying to take our final breath? How many of us have tried to ease the pain by trying to find solace in the depths of despair?

As Twenty-One Pilots says, "Sometimes to stay alive, you gotta kill your mind." And that was all I was trying to do.

For my beloved, affectionately called "kid" Owen, his story was different than mine. He lost his battle with depression in January of 2022. His life was gracious and kind. Funny and exhilaratingly sweet. He was trans. His story is not mine to tell, but I will hold space for his life as long as I breathe. His life affected mine. It flows through me like the quiet ripples in the ocean during the night. His life impacted mine.

His life was meant to continue.

Owen was 23.

How many Owens do we have to have before we make laws to help our trans, non-binary and gender non-conforming youth to show they are loved and protected and adored? How many more Owens do we have to have before we make them feel seen and heard and, above all, given the chance to live? What happens when we love as fiercely as those that hate us? What happens when people put down the hatred spewing in our direction and instead show us compassion and empathy? What happens when we are protected?

Not every story is like mine.

Not every story gets to have a happy ending.

Not every person in my shoes walks out still breathing to fight another day. Self-harm, depression, suicide, anxiety—they're all inherently linked to the anti-trans bills with the LGBTQIA+ community. I could give you statistic after statistic to back this up, but would that change anything?

At what point do statistics equal real lives in your mind?

At what point do people start equating these numbers with real lives?

Because until then, these statistics won't bring change.

THERAPY

I CAN'T PINPOINT the time that I knew I needed therapy as an adult. I think I've always needed it. We all need it, yes, but as a young kid with my biological dad abandoning me, not being able to talk about it or express how I felt about it, knowing I was different from early on—meaning I was not cisgender or heterosexual—I had a lot of pent-up emotions, regardless of whether I could articulately verbalize them or not. As we discussed previously, I had already found unhealthy ways of coping: self-harm, acting out, holding a pistol in my mouth. None of which were healthy in the slightest.

I started therapy when it was school mandated. This is where my therapy journey begins, as I told you already.

But before we get into my journey, I want to pause and say that I know therapy isn't always readily available to everyone—systemic racism, poverty, privilege—those all come into play when we discuss affordable healthcare. Therapy is, unfortunately, a luxury most cannot afford.

The statistics around untreated mental health due to lack of affordable healthcare is asinine, yet that's the state of our country. Until we get universal healthcare, a lot of people will go undiagnosed, therefore, untreated. They will be killed unjustly because cops don't understand and are ill equipped to speak to fellow humans. I could stand on my soap box for years discussing this issue, but it is not lost on me that I am privileged to be able to afford a diagnosis, and yet again, to afford the necessary medication to treat it.

My journey started with school mandated therapy. I know I talked about this in a previous chapter, but I didn't delve into the therapy portion. I was sent once a week to a therapist in the middle of downtown Yadkinville. I don't recall her name. My mom and I kept it a secret from the rest of the family. Even my sister and dad didn't know.

No one did.

We didn't have therapists coming into schools like we have in some states now. It was outside of school hours. I very much thought something was wrong with me. And there was. I was self-shaming. I just didn't know there was a term for it.

I didn't know that it was okay to have mental health issues. I didn't know that so many people have them. I didn't know that so many people go undiagnosed a year for untreated mental health issues—I just knew I didn't want to be different.

I took anger management tests. I was always a head strong kid, and this sometimes meant I acted out or talked back. Looking back, I don't think I needed this test; I think I was trying to get someone to listen to me, and acting out was naturally, what got me the most attention. This is what got me the most eyes on me at one time, and I needed that. I desperately needed someone to hear me for what I couldn't or wasn't allowed to talk about.

I needed someone in my corner, truly.

I took another test that basically determined I was

bordering clinical depression. I was thirteen, y'all. She didn't want to put me on medication, per se, but herbal medications. I was vehemently against any type of medicine, as I watched my mom take so many due to her Multiple Sclerosis diagnosis. I was so against medicine during that time. I didn't want to rely on it. It was a long time before I would admit I truly needed help in the medication form. We'll get to that part later, though.

Needless to say, during that stint of therapy, I didn't take the medication. I'm not sure about the conversation I had with my mom. I don't even know why I quit going to the therapist. But I did. And that was the wrong answer to my problems as I struggled with self-harm, suicidal thoughts and tendencies, throughout much of my life. Even now, at thirty-five, I take medicine to keep those thoughts at bay. I rely on them heavily. They're my saving grace. But I'm skipping ahead.

The next time I would darken a therapist's door was after I got out of the Army at twenty-three-years-old. I had so much unresolved trauma, sexual abuse and assault (Yes, #MeToo), my current career had come to a medical halt. I was essentially at rock bottom. A friend at the time was a staunch advocate for mental health and therapy, so I agreed. I made a lot of progress, but again, I refused to take medication.

I only went a handful of times, and then bowed out again.

I would cherry pick problems to discuss and leave what was festering underneath quietly tucked away for another rainy day to deal with within the confines of my own private home alone.

I would take couples counseling with an ex as my last short stint of therapy until I went back three years ago for the final time to truly seek help. And that form of therapy, because of who I went with, was laughable at best. Nothing to the therapist's fault, it was just a waste of time.

This time, in 2019, I went into the Veteran Affairs hospital closest to me to seek treatment. (Compared to my new VA in Wisconsin, they seriously need some help too, but I digress. That's a whole other book.) I knew I needed help. When you see your primary care physician at a VA, you are always given a questionnaire about your mental state. I answered honestly and was promptly escorted to the Mental Health portion of the VA where I began my mental health journey. I spoke with an interim, and then my counselor, who would become the point of whom I would talk to every other week, once a week. That day marks the day I knew I needed a change in my life. It was the single greatest, yet hardest, day of my life.

Admitting I needed help, and then receiving it.

I still struggle with relying on pills every day. Some days they're just hard to swallow, quite literally. I feel like I'm choking, but I know without them, I'm just a shell of a person. They help me live authentically myself, without the fears creeping back in. Without the shadows in my mind dancing to their own music.

Getting mental health help also afforded me the ability to realize I have an inoperable (for now) brain tumor. It's a cavernoma malformation in the left frontal lobe of my brain, right behind my left eye. Because I spoke up and got help, and my doctor listened to me, we were able to create another treatment plan for my tumor as well.

Mental health is vital to our health and should be treated just like a broken bone. If something feels off, seek help. I cannot stress that enough. If you can afford it, go.

This is your reminder to take care of yourself always.

DON'T ASK, DON'T TELL

I'VE STRUGGLED WRITING this chapter. I wanted to leave this chapter out completely, to be honest with you. I'll be as transparent as possible with you, while still handling the grief that is this chapter. The traumas of #MeToo that are often categorized into the confines of cisgender and heterosexual relationships but fail to leave out the LGBTQIA+ community in all their many facets, is palpable. Couple it with the debilitating fact that I lost an important part of my life is something that leaves me questioning much of my life. But here we are.

Before I get to Don't Ask, Don't Tell, though, I need to back up a bit.

Her name was Angel. We met at a women's only campsite in Virginia. A friend at the time used to bring me there on the weekends. It was an amazing place. Acres upon acres of land. Everything was built by women: the cabins, the outside bathrooms, everything, and eventually, I took part.

I had my hand in helping build an indoor bathroom, re-shingling a house. I helped do a little bit of everything from hammering a nail to sound engineering and assisting musicians at their music festival held every May. I cut down trees, made campsites. I was a baby Jack of all Trades, eventually. I was truly a lumberjane.

That's where I met Angel. A few years my senior. I'm not sure how we met or who introduced us. I think it was a combination of the fact we were the youngest two there and just mutual friends, so over time it was just bound to happen.

But alas, there we were, thrown together like magnets, bound to break apart if turned the wrong away. Like oil and vinegar. We never should've been together. And yet there we were. To say it was a tumultuous relationship from the beginning would've been an understatement, and yet, that was us. Thrown together anyway.

We dated for a while, maybe a couple months, and eventually, I moved to Virginia to be with her. Much of the mundane details are hazy over a decade later, but I know we met about a year after I came out, so around summertime. Eventually, I moved toward the end of that summer. Finding someone who "loved" me was something I desperately craved.

It was exhilarating at first. Let's not speak of the fact we were already throwing those words around, that young, that soon. I was twenty-one, and it was also the first time I lived away from home. Literally everything was new to me. A serious girlfriend, although I had two short relationships before this one, moving away from home, living with someone; it was just *new* everywhere I turned. It was a chance for me to start again, but I didn't know in what context that would soon come to me.

We quickly fell into an extremely unhealthy routine. I wasn't working, had no car to my name, no money to my name. I had nothing but a carload of clothes and miscellaneous books and that was it. I got an interview somewhere and she told me no because it didn't align with her work schedule. And so, I never worked. That should have been a major red flag for me. But I was young, and I didn't know what to look for.

I didn't know the signs.

Folx, this is what we call toxic. She was controlling, emotionally abusive, mentally abusive, and later, would turn physically abusive. It didn't start out this way. We had fun—we were the typical younger couple that went out—we drank a little, we read a lot, we listened to music, we hung out with friends. She was extremely family oriented (hers only), so we spent time with her family, and since mine was in another state, it was incredibly easy for her to isolate me from them, especially without a car to my name.

This is how it started, the controlling behaviors. I don't think it was necessarily that she didn't like my family per se, it was just that she wanted control. Thus, it was harder to talk to them; it became harder to see them, until eventually, I didn't. I barely spoke to them, much less saw them four and a half hours away. It became increasingly difficult.

The same could be said for my friends back home, too. She despised them all. Every. Single. One. Everyone in my life back home she couldn't stand. And yet, I still didn't see these as red flags. As hardheaded as I was, I was the one being controlled.

And I didn't know it.

No one around me told me if they saw an inkling of what was happening. Everyone stayed quiet. I was alone. This was my first time experiencing what it truly meant to be alone surrounded by people.

I can recall two of my friends driving from North Carolina to get me one time because I needed to be home for a surgery my grandpa was having, and she was so rude to them. We're talking, speaking disrespectfully about suicide after knowing that my friend's father lost his life to, to her face. It was cringe-worthy. Looking back, maybe it was she was insecure. Maybe it's because she really didn't have any friends.

There were tell-tale signs, but I was so young. I didn't know what was happening other than I could do nothing right.

I was stuck in every way imaginable.

I moved out once. It was only a couple months into living there. I called a mutual friend of ours and left while she was at work. I thought I could get away. I moved to the campsite where we met. I lived in a camper for about a month. It was the loneliest I had ever felt in my life.

I had nothing.

I also felt like I had no one. I was secluded from my family, my friends, they were all so far away. I was estranged from my entire life. This is what happens when you're in a toxic relationship. This is what they don't tell you.

How quickly it all happens.

How alone you feel.

How alone they make you feel.

How they tear you down and all you have left is the pieces of you scattered about.

When someone speaks about being in an abusive relationship, it never starts that way. It's gradual. They chip away at you daily. It may start as verbal. Saying things like, "What is wrong with you?" *Nothing is wrong with me.* "You're overreacting." *No, I'm not.* "You're the problem." *What am I doing that's so wrong?* It escalates over time, but not in ways you notice. They chip away slowly at your exterior until you actually start to think you're the problem. Until you're thinking you're not good enough. Until you're walking on eggshells in their presence trying to make sure they stay happy; that you do absolutely no wrong. Let me tell you, my friends, nothing you do will ever be good enough for these types of people.

You get to a point where you question yourself at every turn. "Am I doing this right?" "Will this make them happy?" You lose so much of yourself in the process. You lose your will to live. You lose so much weight.

About a year in, though, she became verbally abusive in front of friends. It escalated into talking down to me in front of people. She became intolerable. It was embarrassing.

We bought a house that needed a little TLC. We were upstairs in the bedroom one night talking about painting the walls and an argument ensued. I had had enough. I was finally finding the courage to speak about what was bothering me. I don't remember the exact argument, or how it started, and at that point, it could've been a miniscule thing that I "had done wrong." It just boiled over. I spoke my mind, and the next thing I knew, I was in a chokehold against the wall. I was petrified. Never had I been in an abusive relationship.

I knew then I was fucked.

I don't remember how the argument ended. I just remember being slammed against the wall; her hand wrapped around my throat. Yelling.

The yelling.

It was incomprehensible. I don't remember anything but the feeling of being stuck. I had no one. Nowhere to go. I was officially at rock bottom in my life at twenty-two-years-old. I had just come out two years prior, I should've been living my best life.

Instead, I was being abused in every way.

The next day, I called a friend. It had been my lifelong dream to join the military. I come from a long line of military personnel. I knew I wanted to serve my country. She took me to the Army recruiter's office. We talked. I did the paperwork, spoke to them about what I wanted to do, took the proper tests at Medical Expenditure Panel Survey (MEPS), and signed my name on that dotted line that doesn't expire. Three weeks later I was active duty, in One Station Unit Training (OSUT) in the Army in basic training in Fort Leonardwood, Missouri.

I wish I could say that was where we ended. Sadly, I was also part of the population that believed her when she said she would change. Those three weeks we spent together before I left were amazing. No fights. No drama. It was like nothing ever happened. And for a while, even though I was approximately eighteen hours away in basic training, it seemed like things were finally changing for the better. We were communicating the way a healthy couple should be.

But there was a catch.

Remember at the beginning of this chapter I told you I served under Don't Ask, Don't Tell? That meant you could get dishonorably discharged, aka kicked out, for being LGBTQIA+ in the military. Which also meant, my super looking gay ass, yet again, had to go back in the closet.

Now I know you don't know what I look like, but I'm androgynous to a fault. Short hair, society's definition of masculine clothing, I carry a wallet in my back left pocket. I'm what you call a stereotypical white androgynous person. My hair was not in regulations, which is to say it is shorter than the regulations allowed for AFAB (a female at birth), and at the time, there were, and I'm pretty sure still to this day, only the societal sexes allowed to serve: male or female.

Communicating with Angel was tricky. Yes, we still communicated. Remember when I told you things were smooth after I told her I was leaving for active duty? I had hopes that she had turned a new leaf. I didn't realize how wrong I was, though.

We had nicknames on the phone, abbreviating to our initials in letters we sent back and forth. Any wrong move on either of our part could lead to me being kicked out of the Army. It also meant that I couldn't be authentically myself to the people who were supposed to be family. Anyone could turn me in if I opened my mouth and spoke the truth.

I had to live a lie every single second of every day.

Not letting anyone too close. It was again a lonely point in my life. I couldn't trust anyone with my life, yet those people surrounding me, I had to trust with my life.

There was one time in particular though that I knew I was going to be kicked out.

For anonymity, I'll leave the Drill Sergeant's name anonymous, and just call her DS. At night, we had some down time in our bunks to write letters, sleep, read, study, etc. I fell asleep writing a letter to Angel. It was telling in the letter that I was gay.

During the nights, the DS working nights could flip our bunks. For example, they could completely destroy our bunks and lockers if left unattended and unlocked, and that's exactly what she did. Waking up, I quickly realized my letter was not where I fell asleep with it—it was on the windowsill, flipped to the second page. I have no idea if it was read. Looking back, probably not, but at the time, I was scared out of my mind.

I had been got.

That was it.

My secret was out, and I would be kicked out of the Army for being gay.

That was one of the scariest moments of my life. I couldn't look that DS in the eyes for fear she would make a fool of me in front of my entire company. I was afraid.

Don't Ask, Don't Tell was put into place in 1994 and

lasted until 2011. An incredulous policy that harmed more people than anything. Another policy harming the LGBTQIA+ community. Another policy policing the queer community for no reason other than a fear mongering tool because of the societal unknown.

And there I was caught in the middle of living my truth out loud and being forced back into the closet. I was caught in the riptide of policy and authenticity. I was escaping an abusive relationship by going so far back into the closet that I was on the cusp of finding Narnia. One lonely feeling replaced by another. The whirlwind of serving under DADT was something I will never forget.

I worked hard, I graduated Advanced Individual Training (AIT), earned my designated job title, but fell flat when I injured myself and missed out on an opportunity to deploy. After months of rehabilitation, I was medically discharged for a service-connected injury. Again, another failure in life, it seemed.

It was incredibly disheartening. I became a disabled veteran at twenty-three-years-old. On top of this, Angel had dumped me while still in FLW (via text message), what we call a Dear John letter, on my birthday right before I was getting discharged. Come to find out, she had cheated on me with a married man. On top of being a disabled veteran, I was alone, with nowhere to go but home to my parents.

My time in the Army was short-lived. It was single-handedly the greatest accomplishment and achievement I've had to date. It was also the only time I made a ten-year plan for myself. I had my career mapped out. I knew what I wanted. I had it all in my sights to be ripped from my grasp quicker than it's taken me to write this chapter. It was yet another deafening blow to my self-esteem. Tucking my tail in defeat,

I packed up my things in Virginia and went home to North Carolina.

Serving my country will forever be a highlight in my life. I made some lasting friendships that I still hold near and dear to my heart to this day. I still keep in contact with a few of them and love watching their families grow, but the suffocating feeling of not deploying with them, not being by their side, sometimes still keeps me up at night. My dog tags that are still proudly displayed around my neck in the safety of my t-shirt, will forever be something I will not part with.

This singular item showed me more about myself than anything else in my life. The fear of missing out on my job, my calling, will forever be a missed opportunity for me. I will forever be indebted to my comrades in arms for their sacrifices and lives lost. I will forever be proud of what little I did accomplish, as I know it's not something many people choose to do.

Serving under DADT will forever be a lesson for me. This policy is just one of the dozens of examples of discrimination against the LGBTQIA+ community that is now translated to other policies—such as 45's policy to discriminate against the trans community serving, the infamous bathroom bill North Carolina tried to pass, trans athletes competing in sports, gay men not being allowed to give blood because of certain restrictions dating back to the AIDS pandemic.

The list goes on and on and on.

DADT was just one small micro-aggression of not allowing people to live their authentic lives, and I'm still very much saddened that I had to serve my country in silence.

MICKEY

THIS CHAPTER IS the book I thought I was going to write for years. Only when my perspective shifted, through growing up, maturing, therapy and self-reflection, did I realize it should only be a chapter in my story, not the whole book. Metaphorically, literally, physically, mentally, emotionally… I needed to heal from a lot of unresolved traumas that will always remain, to an extent, unresolved, for as long as I live.

Sometimes we don't get closure from people, we create that closure for ourselves for our own peace of mind. This chapter is that closure for me. Writing this will be the hardest chapter I write, but also the most important. It helped instill in me the will to become my own person. It created in me authenticity. It infused self-love, healing, self-awareness and how to rely on myself. Most importantly, it taught me that who I say I am is important, and I deserve to be loved wholly and without reservations. I owe this chapter to myself, not to anyone else. This chapter is for me, because of me. I owe nothing to no one.

This chapter is about, who I like to call, my sperm donor. You know what they say, there's two sides to every story and then there's the truth. I've only ever gotten one side of the story, and while I have information that helps paint that picture from reliable resources I've gathered over the years, I still only have one side of the story. I doubt I will ever get the second side, much less, the truth.

My mom married young, sixteen to be exact. She had me when she was eighteen. He left approximately six months after I was born. The last time I saw him was at my first birthday party.

Back then, we still had parties at fast food restaurants. Mine was at Burger King. Little did I know at just a year old it would be the last time someone who was supposed to love me unconditionally, would leave without so much as a second glance in my direction, only to deny me later in life repeatedly.

The bone numbing realization of that is enough to make me nauseous typing it a lifetime later.

———

I grew up with my dad who raised me and continues to raise me as his own—because for all intents and purposes, I am his. Legally and any other way you want to call it, just not genetically. My sperm donor bounced before I could create a tangible memory of anything other than what regurgitated stories that have unwillingly been passed along to me and have been seared into my memory.

Like I said, it doesn't matter if I want to meet him or not, that leaves something changed within you. That's a hole in your soul you can't really fill. It's an emptiness that can't be explained with words. You can't explain it. Either you feel it by experience, or you don't.

It's like that meme where the person is complete except

for one missing puzzle piece. There's just no other way around it. It isn't something you can fix on your own. It's a hole you can't fill, it's just there, taking up space. You learn to live with it. You learn to grieve at certain times, wipe your own tears, and go on living. It isn't some linear healing timeline that once you reach a certain age of maturity you grow out of. It evolves as you do. You wonder, as you look into the eyes of your bonus children, am I doing enough? Is this right? Your pain evolves into different things. From childhood trauma to adulthood trauma. You learn to grieve differently at different intervals of your life.

You also realize what baggage you're carrying with you as you mature, too. You are constantly asking yourself questions like, "*Is this a healthy way to respond?*" "*Am I pushing people away due to childhood trauma?*" "*Am I allowing myself to be loved?*" You have to check yourself, too.

Sometimes you're the toxic one.

I know at times I have been. Healing isn't always linear. Sometimes we're the problem. Sometimes we allow our past hurts to hurt us in our present.

———

I wasn't allowed to speak about him growing up. I wasn't allowed to ask questions. I was denied the ability to speak about literally half of my existence. This gave me a complex. I had to hide half of myself. I had to hear that I looked like him, I acted like him, I got my athleticism and book smarts from him, but I was still denied the opportunity to speak his name.

This was traumatizing.

It was humiliating.

It was my family saying you look like this person, you act

like this person, but you can't speak of him. It was hearing nothing but degrading things about him, but then the afore-mentioned spoken about you. It was confusing and all consuming. What was I supposed to think? Who was I? Was I going to wind up a deadbeat—in their words—like him?

I know by now you're hating the family that denied me this right. For a long time, I did, too. It fucked me up, for years, well into my adulthood. I grew up hiding half of myself. I grew up ashamed of half of myself. It's not hard to place the blame. For a long time, I did just that. I blamed them. It was all consuming. I hated them for not letting me speak his name.

And it got me nowhere.

For a long time, I blamed everyone in my family who played a part in silencing me. And while I will still always feel some type of way about it, I now know, I can't change that. The only course for me is through it. To speak my life into existence so that others after me can learn and grow in their own lives. To break the generational curses before me and course correct into the healthiest version of myself possible.

I don't hold anger toward my family for the choices they made anymore. This took years of self-reflection, research, and honestly, growing up, to come to terms with this. A lot of tears were shed through this process, and even still it isn't easy. But forgiveness, not for them, but for yourself, goes a long way in your journey to healing. Let this be a reminder that you heal for yourself, not for anyone else.

When I was a kid, I was angry. I wasn't always so forgiv-ing. I walked through life hating everything and everyone. His birthday, Father's Day, my birthday (signifying the last time I saw him), major holidays… all these dates held mixed emotions for me. I'd be lying if I said they still didn't get under my skin at times.

Sometimes I can get through the days untouched by the lack of memories I have with him, other times I'm left paralyzed. It's like a game of Russian Roulette, and the (lack of) memories, the bullets. All these emotions I had pent up with nowhere to place them. I had nowhere to put them down. There's this quote that has always stuck with me because so many people have continuously asked me why I hold on to so much pain.

"You remember too much,' my mother said to me recently. "Why hold onto to all that?"

And I said, 'Where can I put it down?' (Ann Carson, *Glass, Irony, and God.*)

And that's how it was for me. I didn't have anywhere healthy to put it down. So, I clung to it. I clung to the misplaced weight that I had. The weight of the world, it seemed, was on my shoulders. It was lonely. I grew up never feeling truly seen or heard, much less fully loved.

When I was twenty-eight-years-old, I paid a random internet search provider to track him down. Rather than find him, I found instead the wife he later married after the divorce from my mom. They were married for fifteen plus years. She had children, one a year or so older than me, and another, a few years younger than me, from a previous marriage that he raised as his own.

Hearing this hurt me to my core.

He abandoned me but raised children that weren't genetically his as his own.

That depleted me of worth and feeling. She was gracious enough to tell me in the beginning, he denied me, and then she asked, non-maliciously, why I waited so long to seek her out. After showing proof, documentation, etc., we came to terms with the fact that I was stolen an opportunity to grow up with another family. We're still in contact today through social media, albeit scarcely and very much at face value. I still catch my breath when she likes or comments on a post, after so much silence, I forget she's there. Only when she resurfaces, all the pain comes tumbling back down. He robbed me of so much in life.

And I'm reminded of that with every comment and "like."

It's taken this long to wrestle with the fact that I also gained so much from his absence. I gained a dad who loves me unconditionally. I gained a life. Who knows what would have happened had he stayed? That is a miracle I am thankful for every day after seeing his record. I do not use the word blessed, but I am grateful. I'm lucky. I'm absolutely positive my life is better without him in it. Yet, still, unanswered questions remain.

I can remember writing journal entries and poems to him. I would write down songs that made me think of him. I would tirelessly look for quotes that made me think of him and fill notebooks full of song lyrics, quotes, poems, et al., that gave the slightest inclination of an unrequited father's love and longing for him to come fill that empty void. I would eventually get tired of seeing these sad journal entries, rip them out of my journals, in essence removing him from my life to "start clean," only to start yet another journal about him months later. Repeat infinite.

This has gone on my *entire* life.

I have filled journals just to scrap them. I'm currently looking at ripped pages of songs, quotes, and open-ended letters that's in the back of my current journal to him that will never see the light of day again. I suppose this is what happens when you're left with a hole you can't quite fill. You write it out. You hope by some miracle that writing about it will cure your soul, and maybe that's what my hopes are; maybe that's what I'm doing now.

I now have one specific place for all these things. It's an old black laptop case my late Grandpa gave me. It holds all his arrest records I so tirelessly copied from those paid websites. It has love letters written between him and my mom. It holds pictures of us when I was just a newborn. It holds journal entries and poetry. It holds songs and quotes. It holds notebooks of my paternal lineage I've pieced together over the years. Addresses, phone numbers, e-mails I've all tried to reach him at before giving up completely. Wondering for years since I came out if he would accept me as I am or would be like the rest of my family and force me to hide within the constraints of preconceived boxes.

I tell you this history because it matters.

So often as LGBTQIA+ we have to shrink or hide parts of ourselves in order to feel loved and valued by our families, friends and loved ones. For so many of us, we must hide bits and pieces to make it easier to live in a world that is judgmental. As I'm writing this, in 2021, the United States is on track for it to be the deadliest year for hate crimes in the trans, nonbinary and gender non-conforming community. Add in intersectionality and the statistics grow significantly. Black trans women are the most targeted of this group.

Let that sink in.

We, they, are not safe.

Growing up already hiding half of myself, I had the predetermined notion half of me wasn't worth loving. Coming out, I felt like even less of me was worth loving. That took a major toll on my mental health. Thinking more than half of me wasn't worth even speaking about, let alone being loved, was grounds for a major breakdown.

And friends, a breakdown was what was going to happen.

I just didn't know what form it would take on. Alcoholism played such a major catalyst for my twenties. Drowning myself in sorrow disguised as a ruse for having fun seemed to be all I was capable to doing.

This chapter is still being written. I'm not sure how the ending will go. I know that whatever may come of this chapter will be met with healing and a lot of forgiveness. Not for him, but for myself.

I now know this is just a chapter and not the whole book.

That alone took years to discover.

SHELBIE & MO

I MET my paternal grandmother and great grandmother when I was in eighth grade, roughly twelve or thirteen. So, 1999-2000 time frame, we're talking. Coming from a small town, I was able to run freely through the neighborhoods with my German Shepherd, Sydney. And we would run almost every morning before school. Sydney and I would run by their houses every morning… for almost three years straight, and I had no idea until that day we drove to their house.

I froze when that time came.

Earlier that month my best friend at the time had seen the cuts on my arms and, as she should've, turned me into the school guidance counselor. I knew I needed help, but I had nowhere to turn and the thought of talking to a stranger was terrifying. I suppose that's when my mom knew it was time for me to meet my paternal grandmother and great-grandmother.

The day is gray to me, I don't remember if it was after a school day or on a weekend, where my kid sister was. I just remember my mom putting me in her car and driving for all of one minute down the street.

I looked into piercing blue eyes, bluer than mine, my paternal grandmother's. I don't even remember the quick one-minute drive there. I don't remember if we went inside. I just remember standing there on their sidewalk frozen. I don't remember what was said. Just my grandmother, Shelbie's, eyes. Suffocatingly blue.

I was her duplicate. It's been said, from my sperm-donor's ex-wife, that when my hair was longer, I looked identical to my aunt, Cindy. My eyes though, my eyes are hers.

The feelings that washed over me were fierce. They were a tide, and I was drowning.

I saved pictures from there on out to give to her, but never worked up the nerve to go back. From then, eighth grade, on to my senior pictures, I saved every school picture to give Shelbie. I reckoned that this would somehow make up for all the lost time if I could give her all these pictures. However, that would not be the case.

I only saw her once more before I found out she passed away in 2017. It was at my great uncle's funeral, and she was less than friendly in our short conversation. That was the last time I would see or speak to her. She never got the pictures.

They're still in a small box tucked away.

For what? I'm not sure, I just can't bring myself to process the idea of another loss, I suppose. I can't bring myself to process another relationship I missed out on. I can't process how my family denied my paternal side of the family knowing they lived that close to me my entire childhood.

Some things take time.

And this one is still taking time.

I could say that I'm sad about the last encounter. I could tell you all the things I wish I could've or should've told her. I could tell you I wished on falling stars every time I saw them (even still sometimes to this day, it's the same wish) that

I'd have a chance to be with my paternal family one more time. I could tell you my tear-soaked pillowcases are worn and tattered. I could tell you many things about how I feel, but the honest truth? The honest truth is that my feelings fluctuate daily. It's never the same feeling two days in a row.

Grief is so funny. You'll be enjoying your day and *boom!* It sneaks up on you and you're crying in a Target bathroom. Not that that's ever happened to me.

I have an old, crocheted blanket that Mo, my great-grandmother made. It's my safety blanket. I don't know why I'm so attached to it; it is the most hideous blanket I have ever laid my eyes on, but it's comforting. It could very well be because I knew from an early age who made it, what that meant, and knew one day it would be mine. My mom, for years, even into my adult life, didn't want me to have it for a while. I knew she was waiting until I matured a little, but the attachment was real.

I still cover up with it to nap.

It's in our living room right now.

I find solace in the fact that the kids use it to play with or cover up with. It makes me feel like all the wrongs I had to endure are somehow leaking out with all the love it is now receiving.

DADDY

WITH ALL THE talk of my paternal family, I have my own daddy. Someone I've talked about previously. The very man who adopted me when I was six years old. The one who has treated me like his own since the day he walked into my life as a one-year-old. He will forever be my father. No amount of sperm can counter the love that man has for me. Blood doesn't make us family, but I'm damn sure proud that I can call myself his child.

He came into my life when I was a baby. He's all I've ever known as a father. He tied my shoes; then he taught me how to tie them. He fed me mud pies, claiming they were chocolate. I would sing only around him. He was at every sports game he could possibly attend throughout all my youth. He took me and my kid sister camping. He even gave me my first beer on a camping trip after my sister went to sleep. We stayed up listening to "parental advisory, explicit content" CDs because my mom wouldn't let me at her house. He was there through it all, even after he and my mom divorced, he still was there for me.

He didn't have to be, according to my mom. She told him

he didn't have to pay child support since, by blood, I wasn't his. That, to his account, hurt him. I was his and he was paying for me, too. That was all there was to say about it. Case closed.

My dad is a man of few words. He's laid back. Too laid back sometimes, I think. But it's undeniable how much he loves me and my sister. He's also hilarious. King of the dad jokes and the "that's what she said" moments. He gets to laughing at his own jokes and I swear it's funnier than the original joke. I know you're thinking that I just described every dad in existence, but my daddy is superior, and I'd put him up against anyone.

My mom gave me an ultimatum when I was sixteen. We butted heads a lot. She told me verbatim that if I didn't like living with her, I could call my dad and see if I could live with him. Without hesitation I reached for the phone she held extended toward me, dialed his number, of which I still have memorized all these years later (aren't our memories such erratic things?), and asked if I could move in with him.

That weekend, I was officially living with my dad.

Living with him was perfect. There were no arguments. I kept my grades up, let him know where I was at all times, it wasn't a hard living arrangement. He worked third shift, back then it was 12:00 a.m. to 8:00 a.m., so I would see him after school if I didn't have prior obligations. We would always watch the OG CSI show before he got ready for work. We had our own routine. I lived with him up until I came out and moved in with a bunch of friends.

Even then, I still had my own bedroom and could come and go as I pleased. I didn't, though. I think a part of me was ashamed of being queer mixed with the exhilarating feeling of being queer. And that's just a nuance I can't quite explain. It's feeling so liberated but questioning whether you're still loved (even though absolutely nothing changed with him.) He never once questioned me or made me feel anything but loved and supported. (That's anxiety for you, though.)

My daddy has been there since day one and has not wavered in his support or love in the slightest. I asked him one time to take me to a concert, he never used to take days off, and that was that. He did. We went out to eat and to a Joan Jett, Tesla and Styx concert for my birthday one year. We've sat and played video games for hours while drinking. We're just two overgrown kids and that's a beautiful thing.

He's been steady and loving and while we don't talk every single day, I could pick up the phone right now and say I needed him, and he would be here. I know without a shadow of a doubt that he loves me. And that's another privilege. That I have two parents that love me for me. Not many are afforded that luxury. I'm grateful.

REBIRTH

Sawyer Cole hasn't always been my full government. And while I won't be sharing my deadname, I will tell you how I chose my name. It makes me smile just thinking about my name. Being called my name, receiving mail from partnering publishers for my Bookstagram account or from friends—seeing a text pop up from a lifelong friend using my name—it's like something I can't explain, but I'll try my best.

It's euphoric.

It's exhilarating.

It's acceptance.

It's me.

Every single married woman I know has changed their last name. Dropping their middle name, keeping their maiden name, but nevertheless taking on their spouse's last name. I was met with a lot of pushback when I came out with changing my name. I'm deadnamed by some (and by some, I mean all with the handful of occasional correct names tossed in there if they remember) family members. Some are trying, others are stubborn and refuse to accept my name and are thus no longer part of my story. (Not just because of my name change, but because of several toxic happenstances.) It's never made sense to me, the unwillingness to let someone live their lives authentically in whatever shape or form that may be. In the shadow of a bible, a book that calls you to love one another. A name is a gift from your parents, but if at any time that gift no longer fits, you are free to exchange it. Married folx do it. Who's to say I can't? I grew out of it. It no longer fit.

So, I exchanged it for one that does.

I don't know when I decided to change my name. I always *wanted* to change, though. I have a love/hate relationship with my former first name. I was named after my Memaw, so you can see where I'm going with this. It was an outdated name, but I hold her so close to my heart I never wanted to disrespect her by telling her I wanted to change it.

It took sitting with it to realize that she loves me endlessly. It took me maturing a little to understand that loving her could be separate from holding on to a name that didn't fit. As I type this, she's in a nursing facility battling Dementia, so as far as she knows, and will ever know, my born government is what I still go by. There is nothing more that I want than to share my full self with her, but at this stage in life, I know it would only add more confusion. This will forever remain the only exception to anyone in my life calling me by my deadname.

She is my heart.

And as E.E. Cummings once said, I carry it in mine.

I remember telling my parents on September 14, 2021. (Thank you, text messages that never delete.) I told them via text message, separately. It's always been easier for me to formulate my words (and not freeze from anxiety and panic) to write out what I want to say. I've always been a writer. My dad said, "Okay," like his normal responses to anything.

He still deadnames me.

I try not to let it bother me, but I do cringe inside every time. My mom took it less than okay. Which, now, is understandable. She did give me that name, and I have to allow her space to grieve. She's allowed me space, in due time, to be myself. She calls me Cole and course corrects when she messes up, sometimes. And that's all I'll ever hope for, and maybe one day, there will no longer be a need to course correct; it will just flow effortlessly.

One day at a time.

Choosing my name was a fairly easy process for me. I wanted a name that was gender neutral. I'm trans non-binary, I'm gender non-conforming, so I knew I needed a name that was versatile. I knew I needed, wanted, *deserved* a name that was adequate. I'm androgynous to a fault, so I knew I wanted a name that compiled all these amazing qualities into one. I've always loved the name Sawyer. And since I'm not in the market for birthing or having a child to name, that name was number one on my list. And so, it was meant to be.

Cole was my nickname since I was a teenager. And for the most part, that's what the majority of the people in my life have called me since then. I wanted to keep that because it fit with the aforementioned. It worked. I still go by Cole to my crowd, and I love it, don't get me wrong, but being called Sawyer is a different level of love. It will always bring a smile to my face when I see a piece of mail addressed to Sawyer. It's refreshing. A breath of fresh air. A de-stigmatization of every anti-queer rhetoric I've heard spewed in my direction for over a decade. It's the proverbial fuck you to society's traditional heteronormative exclusive spaces.

And honestly, it fits me.

Sawyer Cole was born after much self-reflection. Sawyer Cole was born like a phoenix rising out of the ashes. A rebirthing. A beautiful beginning. Sawyer Cole was born in the South in spite of, not because of. I'm not telling you the journey is easy coming home to yourself, but I can tell you defining moments like this—like coming home to your name, makes you forget the slander and hatred you've dealt with. Being called by your name for the first time is exhilaratingly beautiful and precious and I really hope you know that feeling. I hope you get to bask in the gloriousness that is you in whatever form that may be.

I can still remember the first signed book I received that was addressed to Sawyer Cole. A book by an indie author I met through book tours on Bookstagram. The feeling of euphoria that is seeing your name acknowledged and in print for the first time is a feeling that just can't be adequately explained, only felt. I held that book for a long time just looking at my name. It was magical.

It still is… Seeing or hearing people use my name. It just never gets old.

FINGERNAIL POLISH

I WAS thirty-four the first time I mustered up enough courage to paint my nails black. For those of you good at math and remembering things, that's right: I was today years old.

A few days before Halloween, at Walmart with my brother, I remember seeing black nail polish and stopping dead in my tracks. My eyes scanned the section as we approached, walking past, and knowing I wanted it. It was an impulse buy; I didn't go there for it, but for some reason, when I saw it, I needed it. And so, on a whim, I scooped it up.

As a young kid, somewhere around sixth grade, my ex-boyfriend's (shudder) sister gave me some. This was during the 90s grunge prime, so my mom was less than thrilled to find black anything in my wardrobe, and naturally she freaked out and took it from me before I got a chance to use it. Despite going through a semi grunge phase, black finger-nail polish was still out of the question. And if there's anyone else out there like me, the more you tell me not to something, the more adamant I become.... I don't care if what you're telling me is the smartest option, I will do the opposite for spite. I am "as stubborn as the day is long," according to my Memaw.

I was never allowed to have black fingernails growing up, long story short. And 90s grunge was the latest "devil's music" of the day. Black anything was not part of the equation. I was so adamant on not being feminine that there came a time I simply didn't want them painted at all. I was staunchly against even the thought of showing one ounce of femininity, black nail polish included.

I didn't want to be a boy, but I was so dead set on *not* being a girl, that I gravitated toward the world's opinion of what "boy" things might include. The vocabulary we have now, we didn't have back then, so "wanting to be a boy" was all that was presented to me.

It's what I thought not wanting to be a girl meant.

I was confused for so long because of this. I didn't have terms like non-binary or gender non-conforming. I never knew what body or gender dysphoria was—it didn't exist in my vocabulary yet.

For so long, I wished not to be a girl. I gravitated toward "boyish" things like toys, clothes, sports. Anything that was designed for a boy by the societal constructs. I wanted to get rid of anything that was feminine about me, my body, or my personality.

Years later, I would learn that I didn't want to be a boy, either.

It was a weird time back then. Not having the vocabulary, we do today, the literature. It was confusing know I had to be one or the other. And since I didn't want to be a girl, the "tomboy" label stuck instead. It took and is still, taking years to deconstruct that notion with my family, that I can exist outside being neither a boy nor a girl. That I can exist as being non-binary. That I can exist being gender non-conforming. That I can exist being trans... without taking testosterone. That I'm perfectly me being trans non-binary.

Where does the black fingernail polish come into play, you ask? Good question. We've conditioned people to think fingernail polish is "girlish." Yes, we see cis het men and nonbinary and genderfluid, and LGTBQIA+ people paint their fingernails more frequently now, but beyond that, we've conditioned ourselves to think one way about certain things— my example is fingernail polish. I thought I had to evade being AFAB (A Female At Birth). I thought I had to disassociate myself completely, in every aspect, to be entirely nonbinary. What a farse.

It's taken me until today years old, when I was at Walmart shopping for Halloween things with my brother, to randomly pick up black fingernail polish. We were in a hurry, passing by the aisles like we were on *Supermarket Sweep*, when it jumped out at me. My eyes scanned each aisle like I was on a hunt to find a hidden gem... and I did. Bottom row, far right, there it sat, like a beacon of light. $1.48 for LA Nails to make me feel a little more like me. $1.48 for something so nefarious to make me feel a little more complete. $1.48 to make me feel a little more like myself. $1.48 to make me feel like I belonged.

I grabbed it on a whim. "Hey, Daniel," I called out. "Want to paint my nails before you go?" Obviously, he was down to do it. My hands shook too badly for me to do it myself, so my affectionate, younger, doting brother stepped in and did them for me. I was pet sitting for my stepmom, so adding something to his agenda the night before they left probably wasn't the best idea, but he made time. Unbeknownst to him, he made time to make me feel a little more seen. A little more myself. A little more complete. $1.48 and a brother to step in and show a little love to his sibling when he didn't have to.

Isn't that what love is? To make you feel a little more complete? To make you feel a little more at home in your own skin?

Fingernail polish is such a silly example of how I'm coming home to myself. But an important lesson for us all to remember. And it took me having them painted, and then sitting with them, and then again later reflecting on why it meant so much to me. On why it was so important for me. Why is such a silly little thing like nail polish so important?

Because I exist outside the binary. Because it's feminine in the eyes of society, and I clearly am *not* in the eyes of the world with short hair and androgynous clothing with a wallet thrown in my back left pocket. Because in a world where there are still aisles for girl and boy toys, nail polish is a reminder that I'm doing something against the natural order of things. My mere existence is against the natural order of things. It's hard to sometimes *just exist*. It takes a lot of effort to live in a world where I'm not "normal." It takes a lot to breathe in a world where it's suffocating with every step you take.

I had hinted for weeks beforehand for my sister to paint them, but she never picked up on it. And I was okay with that, unsure if I really wanted them or not and leaning more toward the latter, but unsure how to approach that topic. I think in the back of my mind, I knew I wanted them painted, but stepping outside of those rigid boxes is still hard. Even the smallest steps for those of us "on the outside" of those boxes, are met with even more skepticism.

"Stop drawing attention to yourself."

"Why do you have to be so different?"

"You're going to get made fun of."

What if, instead of asking those questions or saying those things, we simply let others exist? When one is living authentically, it's easy to appear different. It's also easy to appear like you're seeking attention for simply trying to exist in a world where everyone thinks you must live in some cookie cutter box to belong to the world. What if, instead, we belonged to ourselves and lived happily? What if we existed and let others exist, too? Would that be so hard?

As I said earlier, my sister takes time to process, and with me being trans non-binary, having pronouns that didn't include she or her, and a name change, I've thrown a lot at her in a short amount of time. This doesn't even include what we've experienced as a family in that years' time.

Maybe I'm too forgiving, and I wait too long for people to accept me and love me as whole. Maybe that's still part of my growing process. But to be human is to understand we learn things at different intervals, different time spans, and at different lengths than others. That's what makes us beautiful —the fact that we're all different.

Extending grace to someone takes no effort. I point that out that to say this: malicious intent of deadnaming, misgendering, or causing harm is different than a learning curve that my sister and parents are on. Never once would they do something to outright hurt me, it's just me correcting them until they learn. It's being patient, reminding them from time to time. That's the beauty of love and grace. Malicious intent is when it's done purposefully, like in the case of the rest of my extended family. *That* is when it's not okay. *That* is when it becomes a boundary and mental health problem. I hope you don't confuse the two in your life. It's incredibly tricky trying to find balance within boundaries and grace, but those two can coexist effortlessly when you realize people's intentions.

Even now, when I saw my family off for their Halloween trip, another Republican family member greeted me bright and early that morning, and some of the first words out of her mouth were, "*Deadname*, your fingernails are painted! That's weird. I mean I like them, I'm just not used to seeing you with painted nails."

What a backhanded compliment.

Why can't I, being who I am, have painted fingernails? Who gets to decide that what is okay for one person may not be okay for the next? Why is it socially acceptable for some to paint their fingernails, but not others? These questions all simmered quietly in the back of my throat as I politely smiled and retorted with a shrug and the usual, "I like them," nonchalantly as I sipped my coffee; too early to deal with the intentions of others but smiling nonetheless at my lack of societal life with black fingernails.

I love that I'm androgynous. Sometimes I feel masculine. Sometimes, my mannerisms may come off as feminine. Sometimes, I'm simply neither. And all of those things are okay. All of those things are acceptable. We are all whole as we are, whatever that shape that may be, on any given day, subject to change as we, and only we, see fit. Don't forget that.

MEMAW

ON WEDNESDAY, June 24th, 1987, at 8 lbs., 13 oz., I came into the world with a vengeance. So fast the doctor nearly dropped me, catching me by the neck, breaking my collar bone. To this day, it still shows up on scans.

The only people in the delivery room were my biological sperm donor, my mom (duh), and my Memaw. That's who I was named after, my first name anyway, but you already know this. I think being named after her made us bond in ways she'll never bond with any of my cousins or sister. We were joined together. The link undeniable. The connection tied neatly with an invisible thread that will forever bind us.

This was also why I grappled with changing my first name to Sawyer. I didn't want that bond to be broken. I didn't want her to be upset with me. I didn't want our relationship to be strained. But now, none of that is going to happen.

You see, my memaw is now in a nursing home facing the scary demon called Dementia, like we've discussed. She's the only one who can call me by my deadname these days and get away with it. I don't have the heart to tell her that I changed my name. Not only would she not understand, but she'd also forget, and the conversation would have to be repeated every time we talked, and that's just not something I'm choosing to do. Some days are better than others, but still, that's not a conversation I foresee myself ever having with her.

She's my favorite human to ever walk this planet. My nickname will always be her "angel baby" and she will forever be my North Star.

One time, in elementary school, I was probably about ten, I called Mom from school because I didn't want to be there anymore. I faked sick. She was fed up with my bullshit because I had a habit of doing this. But she picked me up from school and brought me to the emergency room at our local hospital. This is also where Memaw happened to work. Coincidence? I think not. My mom wanted her to call me out on my bullshit, too. Funny thing, though: she didn't.

We had thermometers with mercury in them in those days. And she stuck that bad boy in her cup of coffee long enough to feign a temperature, showed my mom, then promptly took me outside to the drink machine and got me a canned Yoohoo and giggled all the way. She was truly my ride or die. She pulled shenanigans *for* me.

She would do anything for her grandkids. Any of us. But I was labelled the favorite. I was the chosen one. Maybe it was because I was the (self-proclaimed, but true) bastard child who grew up without their biological father, but something about me and Memaw just clicked. From a young age, I only wanted her. I only wanted to be with her. From sleepovers to staying with her throughout the day when I wasn't in school, we were two peas in a pod. So much so that she wanted my mom (who had me when she was eighteen) to give up custody.

I was the middle of the grandkids, it's worth pointing out,

and she never tried this tomfoolery with my aunt about her two oldest kids, so I was truly the one who could do no wrong. I was unstoppable with her beside me. Obviously, my mom didn't give her custody (I would've been in the deep throws of evangelicalism by this point), but it's worth pointing out again just how far she would go to try and get me with her. It was borderline unhealthy, but still, I was the favorite.

Memaw came in clutch for me all the time. She was rock solid. Fighting with cousins? No problem. I always won because I would tattle. Yeah, I was a snitch, but I got my way. So sue me. I was spoiled. Smiling as I write this, I don't think I ever lost a fight at my Memaw's house. I was just that much of a spoiled brat. I'm telling y'all, our first names linked us. No one else had a nickname. *Shrugs*. Favorite.

As I grew up, I didn't spend as much time with her as I had when I was a kid. Just a natural part of growing up, but I always, *always* made time for her when we saw each other at family events. I've never been too old to sit in her lap and get the best hugs.

Especially in the fall of 2015. She had just been to a doctor's appointment when she got to feeling sick. At this point, I was living in Charlotte, approximately an hour and a half away from my family, dating the one that I mentioned earlier about taking couples therapy with.

I picked up the phone late one night, probably around 9:00 p.m., to call one of my aunts and tell her a funny joke—I can't recall now what it was, something about her son, my cousin, I'm sure. But when she picked up the phone, I was met with a rushed tone that she was with Memaw and she wasn't feeling well.

I knew it was serious. I asked if I needed to make the drive back home. She was hesitant but didn't say no. I knew at that moment; I would be making the drive as soon as we hung up. She told me to pick up a thermometer on the way. That night was the beginning of a long year for me.

I got there right at the same time as my other aunt. We literally pulled in one right after another. It took some finagling, but we finally convinced Memaw to go with us to the local emergency room. She was determined to stay at home—that was just the type of person she is—but three against one? She didn't stand a chance.

Things get hazy for me after that. I remember the doctor looking at my aunts and whispering that they needed to go to the hospital in a local nearby town. The diagnosis?

Most likely cancer.

Stage 3C colon cancer to be exact.

We wouldn't find that out until much later in the morning, though. They ran their tests, and by then, my mom had been notified. The family was called awake as the matriarch lay suffering. It's truly the most painful thing in the world to watch someone you love lie there in pain and not be able to help them. What lay ahead would prove to be the most challenging, though, not only for Memaw, but for us as an entire family.

I don't think anything unified us more than her diagnosis, but it also caused forced proximity between those that caused me the most harm. Looking back, I wouldn't change anything I did or the sacrifices—including a failed relationship—that I made, but I would go back and set some healthier boundaries between. I was still just wanting them to love me, rather than realizing it would never happen.

Memaw's journey home wasn't an easy one. Although she would never truly return to *her* home, but to my oldest aunt's house. Throw in an ileostomy bag, chemo, and a year later, all of these things rapidly sped up the Dementia we long since knew she had. It was, more or less, confirmed.

As a family, the three sisters, my mom and two aunts, decided that what was best for Memaw, since she needed around the clock care, would be a nursing home. They chose one and we moved her in. That was probably one of the worst days of my life. I have pictures of me sitting on her lap throughout childhood, even into my adult life, and even through those moments, I've never seen her so… frail. At that moment, not during the surgery or chemo, at the moment of her moving into a nursing home, I knew we had arrived at the final stage.

And that hit hard.

Memaw is truly my lifeline. She's my saving grace. My namesake even if I changed it.

I call her once or twice a week now. It's usually the same conversation: Where I live, I'm in school, what I'm in school for, what I'm going to do with the degree. It's a never-ending cycle of the same questions and answers.

Some days are better than others. Some days she's confused, but it's always a good day when I say, "Hey Memaw," and she responds with, "Hey, angel baby."

My world will shatter when I no longer hear those words.

BOOKSTAGRAM

BOOKS HAVE ALWAYS BEEN a way for me to escape. I joke with my mom that the reason I love to read so much is because I stayed in trouble as a kid, and as a result, the only things left in my room were my clothes and books. (No joke, I even had my door removed once when I got home one day.) And while that's not necessarily wrong, I've always just loved to read.

I would read anything I could get my hands on, even my mom's age-inappropriate V.C. Andrews' *Flowers in the Attic*. I would devour anything set before me. *Goosebumps* to Stephen King to Dan Brown, I would read it all. I would feast my eyes upon anything that would capture my attention. And that was any and everything.

Although I'm a little more reserved to an extent now, I'm always willing to step outside of my comfort zone to read if my trusted friends suggest something.

When the pandemic hit, I was furloughed in late March for a while, for roughly six months, and then later that June found out I was let go. I quickly found a lot of time on my hands. I hadn't yet started school, we all know the world was shut down, so I succumbed to social media influence. Actually, I don't even know if it's even right to say I was influenced.

On a whim, after talking to my sister, I decided to start a Bookstagram account (on Instagram) to review books I read as a hobby to pass the time. I didn't know it was called Bookstagram at first. My sister said I should start a page just for books. I was sure my friends and family were tired of seeing posts every day about the books I was reading, so why not? This was the outlet I never knew I needed. I had no idea what I was signing up for, or the lifelong friendships and relationships I would make along the way.

Bookstagram, for those of you who may not be familiar with it, is a facet of Instagram dedicated solely to reading and reviewing books. It's a community. A huge community of nerds, and I love it. We share our love of reading, some of us are partnered with book publishing companies where we read Advanced Reader Copies (ARCs) or Advanced Listener Copies (ALCs) before their release date and post our reviews about them. Some of us have partnered with bookish apparel companies, candle companies; you name it, there's a niche for everyone. It's a community of readers united by one singular thing: the love of reading.

It's also a place to grow as a person. I've learned so much by being in that space. I've learned to expand my intentional reading. I've learned more about cultures and traditions. I've learned more about myself. I've created an independent book club. I've dropped a merch line for said book club. I've partnered with some amazing small businesses ranging from book subscription boxes to candles, to bookmarks to clothing companies to actual publishing companies.

I've truly grown exponentially. The people within that community have taught me so much. From reading intentionally—meaning reading outside my chosen genres of memoir or queer to reading Black women, Indigenous women, BIPOC, AAPI—it's ensuring I read marginalized communities other than my own.

I'm part of an amazing group who is self-deemed as "The Anchovies." A pod, or a group, of fantastic humans that constantly lift each other up. There's roughly twenty of us, give or take a few. A group that has become more like family than strangers on the internet. (Looking at you mom, who said not to talk to strangers online.) A group that is full of the most bizarre conversations to serious, in-depth talks and pep talks that leave me filled, replenished and whole. A group of crazy assholes who do nothing but shit talk and are there for each other, through the death of animals, family members and even there for the occasional day-to-day crises to silly TikTok videos, and of course, book recommendations.

When people tell you that you can't *possibly* love strangers like you would someone you know in real life, they clearly have never met *this* group of people. A group that feels more like family to me than my own family. A group that encourages, uplifts, and is there for you in a time of need, that has proven time and time again. A group of people who will travel sporadically to spend time with one another *just because*.

This chapter is vital to my life because through my pronouns, coming out as trans non-binary, my name change, they were there every single step of the way cheering me on. Those fools are family. During all those times, never once was I questioned, ridiculed, or treated any differently than from a place of love and adoration. Never once was I treated like an afterthought. They always came ready and willing to learn and understand if they didn't and figuring out ways to encourage me along my journey. Just as I do to them along their journeys.

People talk about finding your people often. They say it's better to have quality over quantity, and they're right. It took me so long to find my people. Especially when I needed them. Aside from my in real life best friend, I had no one 100% in my corner who encouraged me, accepted me, gave me room to be myself and respected me until I met that group. I've made no efforts to hide the fact I've felt alone most of my life. I've made no promises that this life of mine has been easy to manage. But with the right group of people in your corner, you feel unstoppable. You feel like you can conquer the world.

And you don't feel so damn alone.

I know I haven't since I met them. I know they've often-times been where I go when I just need to escape real life, regardless of whether they know that or not.

Aside from this incredible group of "Anchovies," I've also met some amazing people through Bookstagram. I could begin listing names, but the fear of leaving someone out far outweighs my need or want to name drop. Some smaller accounts, some bigger accounts, all still beautiful people behind the numbers. All people that have helped shape me into the person I am today, who have sent me books, kind words, lent their ears or offered supportive encouragements along the way.

One of which, though, has basically held my hand through this writing process. One who has turned into more like a sibling than a friend or stranger on the internet. One that drove hours to meet me once I moved to Wisconsin so we could become more than just "online siblings" but real-life ones, too. One I will forever be indebted to for my endless pestering questions, whining and overall help in overcoming my imposter syndrome. One that helped me through this process while writing her own books. One who has been there through my name change, pronouns and the like, as well, who sent me her cap and gown so I could wear it for a surprise graduation party they all threw for me online.

That kind of friendship is rare.

But you come across them in the unlikeliest of places. Bookstagram is it for me.

Now I'm not telling you to make a Bookstagram page (I mean, you're missing out if you don't, but whatever), if reading isn't your thing (it should be). What I am telling you is that you're never too old to find your people. Sometimes you get lucky, and you grow up with all your people.

My very best friend I've known since I was nine years old. I got lucky with that one. But I am telling you to be open to new experiences. I'm telling you to take chances. I'm telling you to look for the positives wherever you go. I made a Bookstagram page to discuss books, and it turned into so much more. I found unwavering support and comfort in a time in my life when I truly needed it. I found a group of people who are so good at uplifting that I feel comfortable in sharing my unfiltered thoughts as they come into my brain.

I'm telling you that your people are out there. Don't think that you have to have all these nights out with people to find your people. I found mine in the comfort of my own home, online. Who's to say if we'll ever meet up. We've all discussed it. I'm sure it will happen eventually. I'm also sure there will be a novella about it somewhere. You will find your people in the most unlikely places, when you least expect it. You just have to be open to taking chances and trying new things.

I made my Bookstagram account to find comfort in the unknown. To have a creative outlet as a hobby. And now, I find comfort in the fact I have a group of people surrounding me that will come to my defense quicker than it takes you to read this sentence.

It's all about taking chances.

Trusting people.

Trusting the process.

Diving in headfirst into the unknown.

I also met my fiancée through Bookstagram. That woman slid into my DMs like she was a damn professional. It took weeks for me to figure out I was being hit on. I'm not sure if she was slick with it or if I'm *that* unaware of people hitting on me (she'll vote the latter), but there we were. It started out as innocent shit talking and escalated into the beautiful relationship I have now, and I will forever be thankful. We'll touch more on this particular subject later, but just know, for future reference, that I met the love of my life on Bookstagram, too.

Again, I'm not saying your people are on the internet. I'm saying almost all of mine were. I'm saying your people, maybe even your significant other, will be in the unlikeliest of places if you're open enough to allow things to happen. If you go through life with your head down, you miss out on so much. If you go through life and don't take chances, or create new things, you miss out on the communities that connect you to your passions in life. You miss out on community. You miss out on new opportunities to grow as a person and grow *with* people.

So take chances.

Follow your dreams.

Your hobbies.

You never know what path they may lead you down.

Follow your passions in life. You have no idea where they will take you or the people you will meet along the way. Don't be brash in your decisions but figure out what sets your soul on fire.

Definitely do more of that.

You never know where life will take you when you follow your heart.

BOOKS

I READ a quote once that said there is no friend more loyal than a book. And as I recall that quote, I can't help but think it still rings true. I love my best friend more than anything in this entire world, but I get lost in books. It's a different type of loyalty. It's the comfort in the unknown. Be it happily ever afters or world building or memoirs, there's no type of loyalty quite like a book.

Books have been my escape since the beginning of time. Okay, maybe I'm exaggerating a smidge, but they have been my escape since I was a wee little tot. My mom told me she read the encyclopedia to me when she was pregnant with me. There were quite a few books I remember strongly from my childhood that she read to me growing up. Books I still own. Books of which are tattered and torn, and the covers have either fallen off completely or are well on their way.

Books are why I created a Bookstagram page... where I met my fiancée... no one can prove to me that books can't change the entire existence of your life. It sure did mine.

When someone asks me what my favorite book is, these are the steps I painfully go through:

1. I freak out internally. I'm talking, I forget every book I've ever read.
2. I forget how to speak. Words? Never heard of them.
3. I also forget that I know how to read.
4. I get pissy that someone would ask me such an impossible (stupid) question.
5. I begin to recall books and name only the first one that comes to mind.

In all seriousness, the one book I will always give you, though, without a shadow of a doubt, is *All Boys Aren't Blue* by George M. Johnson. Their book, I could write a book about. Go buy it. (Please finish mine first.) You know what, or not, just read their book. Okay, and scene.

Books come in many facets, and I've read them in many forms: audio, paperback, hardback, e-book, advanced reader copies, I've devoured them all. No form is superior to the other, either. Don't let anyone tell you any differently. I can read quicker with e-books but prefer paperbacks. Want to know a secret? I will fold that bad boy back and read to my heart's content. Cracked spine? Whoops. As Tab says, "That's my business."

Books give you some place to go when you can't leave where you are. They give you a means to escape. They give you solace when you're sad. They're a familiar hug when you need a friend's embrace and have no one around. They provide you with an endless amount of travel right at your fingertips. All you need is your imagination. You can't tell me books can't change the world.

Books offer you friendships. They listen to you. They catch your tears. They offer you guidance if you listen long enough.

Books will always be my first best friend.

Maybe it's because as a kid I stayed grounded and had everything taken away, so that's what I was left with.

They were there when no one else was.

They'll remain there, too.

REPRODUCTIVE RIGHTS

As I sit here writing this, it's been leaked that SCOTUS will overturn Roe v Wade. For people with uteruses, this is a huge blow to our reproductive rights. For a trans non-binary person having a uterus, this petrifies me. What will happen next? Will my trans-ness be too much? Will the ability to get gender-affirming care be stripped away completely? What about being non-binary? What will happen to my pronouns? I know they won't just magically disappear, but using them—will they be frowned upon by society even more than they are now? Will they be outcast and paint a target on my back more than the one I already have?

I already fear using public restrooms and fitting-rooms. Where does that leave me being so open about what I am within my exterior looks? I'm a target by that alone. What happens when I see my primary care physician? Will I be turned away? These questions, the majority of the world don't even think twice about... yet here I am. Worrying about my sheer existence in a world by one SCOTUS ruling. It's terrifying.

It's like we're crying in a language no one wants to understand.

It's like we're evaporated from everyday life.

Let's still not forget the intersectionality that comes into play here. I have the fact that I'm white in my favor. Black women and Black people with uteruses have been systemically left out of the equation far longer than anyone else. That should not go unnoticed. Or uncorrected.

People of all genders have abortions. Correction—they *should* have access to affordable healthcare. No matter what. This should be the law of the land, yet here we are. Fighting for our rights to just simply be, yet again.

For trans people, non-binary people, and people all over the gender spectrum, we're often erased from feminism. And as I've stated previously, intersectionality or bust. Your feminism should include those of all genders and ethnicities, in your fight for equality in reproductive rights. We don't fit into the societal definitions of the binary and too often we are discarded, but we are here. We are taking up space and our rights are sometimes the last to be protected. Our rights are integral in the fight for all equality, dating back centuries. Often times, we are on the frontlines *for* you, before you even are.

We're here.

Fight for us too, damnit.

That's what keeps rolling in my mind as I see meme after meme posted about women. "WHAT ABOUT ME?!" I want to yell into oblivion. "What about me," I plead.

When the news broke, I saw on social media, all of it, how we were erased from the conversation. Women this, men that… never about the people with uteruses that didn't fall into the societal construct of the binary. So often, we're just erased completely, like we don't even exist. Even Vice President Kamala Harris, in her robust position in reprimanding the SCOTUS, spoke only of women, which left a sour taste in my mouth. Where are we in this fight? When do we fit into the picture? Does my uterus hold no weight against someone who identifies as a cisgender woman? Where do I fall into the fight for reproductive rights?

Too often we see this. If we fall outside the societal binary of the world, we're misplaced, set aside, forgotten, or altogether just discarded. Which does wonders for our mental health. We're erased from an entire populous of people; yet we're still here. We're alive. We're still fighting.

We're tired.

Tired of being ignored.

Tired of being forgotten.

Tired of being left out.

We aren't trying to erase women's rights. We're the most dependable supporters *of* women's rights. We also know there are more people with uteruses than just cis women. We want to be included into protections you're so fiercely advocating for. We want to be advocated for, as much as we advocate for you. Is that too much to ask? We want to be protected, too.

Maybe this sounds like a desperate plea. Maybe it is. I'm tired. So tired. Because I'm writing this through gritted teeth and tear-stained cheeks as I fear what this SCOTUS is capable of. I'm not dumb enough to think this will be the end of the rights they attempt to strip away. No. They've already started if you want to be technical. Hundreds of anti-trans bills have been brought into, or passed, legislation.

This is just the beginning.

The beginning of the end for a lot of people.

Trans rights are under attack. Trans and gender non-conforming and non-binary kids are being targeted in states

like Texas and Florida. To say it will happen 'next' is a lie…
It's already happening. How can we solve this?

By including us in your fights.

By including us in your conversations.

We've always been here. Now we just have the vernacular
and gumption to be out-spoken by people who have tirelessly
fought for our rights—like the Stonewall Riots. Like the Civil
Rights Movement. Are we going to let that be erased? Are we
going to fall behind yet again? Are we going to go back in
time? This is my whole-hearted plea for you to include us in
your discussions. We see what's happening and we're terrified. We're terrified to step out into the streets. To go out in
public. To use restrooms. To use fitting rooms. We're
constantly looking over our shoulders to ensure we're safe in
our day-to-day activities.

Just like you, women.

We know what it's like to carry our keys between our
fingers when walking across the parking lot. About unneces-
sary name-calling from a stranger in the street. We know
what it's like to have unwanted guests speak about our
appearances.

We understand. We just ask that, in turn, you understand
us.

We're no different, you and me.

We're more alike than you think.

Please fight for us, too.

I turned thirty-five this year. I know you're wondering why
that's important, especially in this chapter. But my thirty-fifth
birthday marked one for the history books, and it wasn't

because of my birth. SCOTUS overturned Roe v Wade on June 24th, 2022—the day I turned thirty-five.

Dare I say a date the world stopped.

People with uteruses collectively stopped breathing at once.

Queer people began questioning how quickly they would bring into question Obergefell v Hodges next. The married queer people began getting their affairs in order considering children, wills and other things afforded to heterosexual couples that could be stripped away with one decision.

This was worth revisiting since my fears initially became reality. I can't imagine being someone with a uterus who wants to reproduce and not having the bodily autonomy to make a choice if things get dangerous for them during the pregnancy. I can't imagine not having bodily autonomy with instances like ectopic pregnancies, miscarriages, or other deadly scenarios in which the birth person is at risk of dying.

This was worth revisiting because there have since been rules to ban LGBTQIA+ books, gender saving healthcare for adults and children alike. There have been laws put in place to force people to carry unwanted or dangerous pregnancies to birth. I can't imagine living in this utopia of a nightmare, and yet, here I am.

This is my last plea to include us in your conversations.

This is my plea to hear our cries, too.

EDUCATORS

EDUCATORS MAKE the world go 'round.

For a long time as a kid, even as a young adult, I wanted to become a kindergarten teacher. I wanted to change the world. I wanted to speak life into existence for little kids, to be that role model for them. The educator that they remembered fondly when they got older and began listing their favorites over the years. I wanted to be that person.

I interned with a kindergarten (and first grade) class during my high school years and quickly found out that I didn't have what it takes to make it as a kindergarten teacher. I was not bubbly—as in, hilariously not at all. And I think those little minds need someone energetic and active and extroverted and theatrical in a sense, but those descriptors do not define me in the slightest. I'm an introvert to a fault and thrive on organization and quiet. These things you will not find in a kindergarten class.

It's also imperative we have educators who *want* to be there. Who are dedicated individuals that want to see their students thrive, not only in the classroom, but outside of it, as well. I know the majority of educators are like this—I speak from experience, from a public education system student perspective—that 98% of these educators put their all into teaching. They go above and beyond to ensure their students get the essentials they need to succeed. They spend money out of pocket every single year for their students. They spend more time at school with their students than at home with their families. They work two or three side jobs to not only support their career as an educator (buying said supplies), but also making ends meet at home. Educators are rock stars, y'all. They are diamonds in the rough. We should be thankful for them all.

When talking about educators, there are two that stand out the most to me through my time in public school. Even though it's hard to choose favorites, because there are so many I could name for a myriad of reasons, these two have gone above and beyond to enrich my life, even as an adult, in every way possible. They have been there to scold me, to educate me, lift me up, support me in so many aspects, and show love their own separate ways. They've been there to guide me, even when I was unaware. They've kept teaching me well beyond the classroom. Through gaining a friendship with them outside the classroom, I've gained role models. This is the type of educators we need in the classrooms— those that change lives, not just in the curriculum.

One of them was my seventh-grade health and social studies teacher. He's a local celebrity back in my hometown. Even if you never had him as an educator, you knew who he was. Genuinely a legend in his own right. He is larger than life. He exemplifies what it means to have grace, compassion, stand in what you believe in (even if it means standing alone), to have sportsmanship, to have sound morals… I could list attributes for the entirety of this book, but you get the idea; the man is one of a kind. My hometown is lucky to have him.

He has the best stories you'll ever hear, and he should be the one writing a book, not me. His life is lesson after lesson. He has a story for everything. He will quote lyrics, poems, Greek mythology, or a haiku if it means leading you into a positive head space. He will dress up as Superman, with his sunglasses on, and serenade you with "Happy Birthday" like he did every month in the cafeteria at school. He believes in every single one of his students and truly wishes nothing but the best for each and every one of them. He remembers the names of every single student, their siblings, their parents. He can't even go to the grocery store down the street because it would take him so long to buy groceries because he'd stop and talk to everyone. (Seriously, he goes to another county to buy groceries. Who does that?) He is, and will forever be, a legend. We could all learn to be more like him.

Remember that coach I told you about earlier that was talking about how positive I was for trying at sports and never giving up? This is him. He was the best motivational speaker; actually, he *is*, or at least *was*, a motivational speaker at one point during his life. The man is unstoppable.

He never gives up on people. He will always be there cheering you on, regardless of if you were one of his athletes or students or not. If he meets you, he will remember you. I'm not sure how he does it. And he's completely sincere about it. He genuinely cares about everyone he meets; in all actuality, he cares about people he's never even met. A philanthropist to the nth degree.

He cared about me when I was at my roughest. My mom was diagnosed with MS a year prior of having him as a coach or an educator. By the time I got to him, I was acting out. I wasn't really trying my best. Just doing what I had to do to stay afloat in school. I excelled in sports. I'm athletic by nature, and even then, I didn't make any of the teams (volleyball, basketball, nor my favorite, and the one I'm best at, softball) because I *just didn't care.*

Not making the softball team was my fault, though. I skipped a day of tryouts with my best friend at the time because we thought we were going to make it, so we bailed one day and got busted by the assistant coach. The phone call he made that night to the house was brutal. Not because he yelled. He was cool, calm, and collected. He just called to inform my mom what happened and asked to talk to me. The only thing I remember from that conversation was that he was disappointed, and that hurt worse than anything else. My mom could've grounded me for all I cared, but those words stung. I didn't make the team that year, and I had to live with that. That was my punishment. It was the longest year of my life.

I bounced back, though. I didn't give up. I showed him I wanted it. Not only did I make every team the following year, but I was also a starter. It turns out, years later when I was helping him coach when I was in high school, he presented me with a plaque that showed a perfect defensive record in softball. I held a record dating back to the time that elementary school was a high school. Had I not had him believe in me to try out again, to keep working hard, I wouldn't have come back to hold that record. I still have it sitting out, reminding me that it doesn't matter if I fail—whether I self-sabotage or not—that setbacks are set ups for come backs.

As an adult, behind closed doors, he's also believed in me and supported me. When I came out with my name change, he messaged me on Facebook and asked for my address. A couple days later I received a book in the mail. It was a book explaining how a stoic philosopher named Marcus Aurelius dealt with that "out of place feeling." (Coach's words, not mine.) Even still, he taught me again the lesson of "I'm your teacher forever" (Again, his words) when he sent me a check to go toward my top surgery after I went public with it the following year on Facebook.

He's always pouring himself into his students and athletes. Hell, even strangers. He never does it for show, it's always done discretely. He'll never tell you what he's done for others. He's selfless, and he's taught me more about how to be an upstanding adult and citizen than anyone else in my entire life.

The next educator in my life is a short red headed fire-cracker who is the sincerest woman I have ever met. She was my eighth-grade science and math teacher. My least favorite subjects. I could not tell you one single thing I learned in that class (sorry, ma'am), but I do remember before basketball practice every day going to her classroom to help her grade papers. I remember *wanting* to be around her. Her presence was calming. Don't get me wrong, the lady, as I previously described, is a *firecracker*. She was not afraid to light your ass up if you acted up.

My mom explicitly gave her permission to do so if I acted out. She scared me and remained directly in my line of respect. I did not cross her. I'm laughing now as I write this. I can remember her classroom being directly next door to my English class. It was that old thin carpeted hallway. The long hallway with the counselor's office I told you about earlier. There was a desk permanently outside the English classroom for those of us who acted out. We would get kicked out of class. I lived in that hallway. (Years later, I learned even some other educators couldn't stand that particular educator, she was so bad, but that's none of my business. Wink.)

Anyway, one day I was feeling especially spicy and was showing my ass to my English teacher outside in the hallway. I was being a smartass when all of a sudden, the math/science room door flew open and out walked this firecracker with her finger pointed in my face telling me to behave. "Yes ma'am," is all I'm sure I had the courage to muster. She scared the piss out of me in the best possible way. She demanded respect, and I gave her every ounce. Still do.

I already had a relationship with her before she became my math and science teacher, though. Remember when my mom was diagnosed with MS and my sixth-grade teacher sent me to the eighth-grade teacher? This is the one she sent me to. I remained in contact with her throughout my sixth, seventh and eighth grade years. She answered any and all questions I had because she has someone close to her that also has MS.

One particular year, my mom was put out of work, her disability hadn't been approved yet, she was a single parent, and we had no idea how we were going to pay bills, let alone how she was going to afford Christmas for me and my kid sister. I'm not sure how this educator knew what was happening at home, or how we were rolling change with our mom to pay bills, but her and her husband randomly gifted Mom some money.

It covered some bills and Christmas that year.

Two years ago, she lost her husband. I had no idea how to be there for her, as I had never been married nor lost a spouse, but I knew I needed to do something. I invited her to lunch at a local spot in downtown Yadkinville. When we met, the first thing she did was scold me and told me straight up, as seriously as possible, that if I didn't let her pay for the meal she was going to leave right then. (Told you she was a firecracker.) I laughed, smiled, and said "Okay," thinking that I was just going to grab the check at the end and be done with it.

Easy peasy.

We had our meal. She shed a few tears, but beyond that, we picked up where we left off talking about any and every-thing. What was new in our lives, what we were doing to pass the time, how our families were, etc.

Little did I know our meal would be paid for by a stranger. I, to this day, have no idea who paid for our meal. And I owe it all to the testament of how much she (and her husband who was also super active in the community) played a part in this community. How loved they are. She thought for a while it was me who paid, though. But once she realized I hadn't left the table, she knew it couldn't have been.

I couldn't have survived my angsty, horrible, lonely preteen years without those two educators in my life. I couldn't imagine my life without them as an adult. They are, without a doubt, two of the most influential people in my life from adolescence to adulthood. They're irreplaceable.

Educators are world changers.

They make the world go 'round.

PRIDE FESTIVALS

"THE FIRST PRIDE STARTED AS A RIOT."

WHAT IS A PRIDE FESTIVAL, you ask? A Pride Festival is a (sometimes weeklong) party that includes, but not limited to: a parade, vendors, food trucks, live music, drag shows, night life (bars, clubs, etc.) and so, so much more. It is a place to exist. It is a place free of judgment. It is a place of love and acceptance and belonging.

It is a place of pure, unconditional love.

It wasn't always a time of jubilation and happy times, though. It started as bricks thrown, arrests made, Black and BIPOC trans and gender non-conforming people fighting for their rights to simply exist and cohabitate. In 1969, it was a riot, full of liberation, demonstrations for equality and protests that began in response to a police raid on Stonewall Inn in Greenwich Village. In 1970, however, it turned into a parade. Full of joy and laughter and freedoms. Make no mistake, our liberation, our happiness, our freedoms, started out as a riot against the police trying to control us for existing.

The first Pride Festival that really stands out to me is

Capitol Pride. I went with some friends from Virginia, and we made a day out of it. It was the biggest Pride I've been to. I had been to some smaller ones around my hometown, but never one of this grandeur.

I remember seeing Ru Paul and Ongina from the first season of *Ru Paul's Drag Race*, perform from a distance. It was exhilarating. I'd never been to a drag show before, let alone one of this size, so it was truly breath-taking.

It's genuinely euphoric: the feeling of being at your first Pride. Not because there's so much free shit (newsflash, there is). It's because you are free to be you, whatever that looks like. You can dress up (or down) and be exactly how you feel on the inside. For me, that meant dressing more androgynously. For some, it means dressing in your own gender (not assigned at birth). It's matching your outsides to your insides, and for some, that comes only once a year. For some, it's the chance to try out new things in an environment that won't look at you sideways for dressing or presenting yourself a certain way. It's having the freedoms to try new things in an atmosphere that lets you be you in all your queer glory.

It's a place to feel comfortable. It's welcoming. It's like this huge family that's throwing a party and you're all decked out in rainbows and shit. It's glorious. It's feeling welcomed just as you are. It's reassuring. It's knowing you fit in just the way you are, no exceptions. No one is there asking you why you are the way you are. You're accepted 100% as is, no questions asked. There are people in nothing but banana hammocks and even still others dressed scantily, and no one bats an eye because it's fucking Pride and we all fit in when we stand out.

There's music. There's the free shit I mentioned earlier. There are drag queens and kings and food and drinks, both of the alcoholic and not. There's LGBTQIA+ vendors set up everywhere, ranging from jewelry to accessories to face painting. There's after night parties and clubs. There's drag bunches and lunches and late-night shows. The list goes on depending on how large the festival or city is.

Of course, there are the occasional protesters and picketers. Most often, they're met with Free Mom Hugs, an organization started by a phenomenal lady I'd love to meet one day, Sara Cunningham. Free Mom Hugs started as 'free mom hugs' from moms willing to step in and act as a mom to those displaced in the LGBTQIA+ community who just needed a hug from a mom. It's now expanded to dads, and brothers and sisters, and siblings, aunts, and uncles.

Cunningham championed Free Mom Hugs in response to her relationship with her gay son and it's now this beautiful montage to the love she, and others, have to give to those within the LGBTQIA+ community who may have been shunned from their own family and friends. I know I have personally experienced a Free Mom Hug and it was the best. It's just a different type of hug. It's a different type of love. If you ever get a chance to get one of these, do it. Best decision of your life.

The protesters and picketers, most often than not, are met with tons of people isolating them off from the rest of the Pride Festival. Be it biker clubs, Free Mom Hugs or just random allies, these people do the hard work in shielding us from the hate and vitriol those souls attempt to spew in our direction. Everywhere from bible verses, picket signs telling us we're abominations and going to hell and so much more hatred being yelled, even some with micro and megaphones.

They have no reason or justification to be so hurtful, but they spend the entirety of Pride Festival screaming at us from afar. Some people attending Pride will argue with them, at one time, I was one of them. I was so full of rage that I wanted to scream, and so I did.

It doesn't do any good, though.

That arguing-with-a-brick-wall mentality.

MEDICATIONS

I'M 100% me because I take pills every day. My mental health depends on those tiny, glorious little capsules. My life depends on them, too. I will never *not* take my medicine. I'll be on them for the rest of my life. That is something that I know to be true. While many people choose or have better results from something else, I have better results from medication.

This is my story.

For a long time, I grappled with the sentence *I'll be on them for the rest of my life.* I didn't want to take medication. I barely took ibuprofen for a headache. Very rarely would I take anything, including vitamins. I just didn't want to take pills of any kind. They scared me if I'm being completely honest.

My rationale was thinking that I didn't want to put anything in my body that I didn't know the long-term effects for. Newsflash everyone: I'm in the U.S. and eat crap food and drink crap drinks. So that excuse was just stupid. But for a while, I kept that justification locked tight.

I was genuinely afraid of the unknown. In all honesty, I

also wasn't mature enough to get myself help for my mental well-being. It took me a long time to grow up and put my health first. It took me a long time to realize and accept the fact that I did, in fact, need help. And I hate asking for help. I loathe it entirely. So, to say I needed help on this grand of a scale was something I was not prepared to do. I was not prepared to take medicine. But that's exactly what I did.

I wish I had reached out sooner. I wish I would've asked for help before I was thirty-three years old. I wish mental health was talked about when I was growing up. Sadly, in the 90s, even in the early 2000s, mental health was still very much stigmatized. Hell, it's still stigmatized to this day. If you got help you were weak. It was frowned upon in a sense. You sucked it up and carried on. You didn't speak about things like that. You just didn't. That was how life worked back then.

My mental health journey is unique to me. I know others had parents and family members and care givers that openly spoke about mental health, mental health days and protecting your peace. That just wasn't in the cards for me. I didn't really have anyone in my life to talk about mental well-being. No one was there to guide me in my feelings or why I felt the way I felt.

My journey started young, as you know. I have been in and out of therapy for a long time, but never medicated. It wasn't until I was thirty-three that I began getting serious about my mental health. It wasn't until then that I realized my thoughts were not going to get better on their own. It wasn't until I was thirty-three that I began realizing I needed to ask for help. And so, I did, at the VA.

The process of starting medication can be a daunting task. It's answering all these questions and talking about your innermost thoughts and feelings. It's taking a deep dive into your mind and swimming to shore with the answers you didn't know you had. It's placing words on feelings you never thought you were capable of naming. It's also digging deep into your past and recalling traumatic situations to define why you may be experiencing things the way you are now. It's all an intimidating process, but it can be done.

Once you get past the initial intake questions, life gets a little easier. You begin discussing symptoms and what medications may work for you. You begin examining yourself and how your body reacts to certain medications. It is a process. Just because the doctor may put you on something doesn't mean that a) it's a quick fix and it will magically make everything better b) be the correct dosage or even still c) be the right medication for you due to side effects.

My first medication for depression made me feel absolutely wonky. I was hearing things. Hallucinating. It was scary. I was on the highest dosage possible, and I felt like I was irrational all the time. It made me feel completely illogical and not in control of my own body or surroundings. It was not the medication for me. Luckily, I was in tune with my body and my therapist and psychiatrist listened. It was the scariest feeling not being in control of your own body.

Medication works differently for everyone. It isn't a super quick fix. It takes weeks (read: sometimes months) for medicines to get fully into your system and even longer still to determine if they are a right fit for you or not. It's a grueling process and requires patience. Sometimes, more patience than we are capable of giving, but still have to try to give.

After being diagnosed with bipolar disorder, we decided to try a medication for that, and it worked tremendously. We have upped the medication since then and added something that works to balance out the depressive lows. We have also added something to not only help me sleep at night, but works to help my depression and mood, as well. I take a total of three medications for depression and bipolar. Add another one still for my anxiety. And yet another one for my inattentive ADHD that we're still trying to figure out now. And let's not forget three Vitamin D pills a day because that's low, too.

When you begin seeking treatment for your mental health, that often requires blood work and blood pressure and all sorts of tests to ensure the medication isn't causing your body to go out of whack but also it could lead to more problems being found. Like my Vitamin D levels being low.

Another example of this is the cavernoma malformation they found. A cavernoma malformation is a tumor that is found in your brain. (We'll get to this story later.) They didn't go looking for this tumor, but because I had described symptoms, they scheduled an MRI to rule things out. This is when they found it. On accident.

Because I was vocal about my mental health, because I spoke up about how I was feeling, because I continued to express myself, they took me seriously and scheduled a test to solve the problem. I found my tumor (which is now monitored) because I sought out help for my mental health. The two inexplicably go hand in hand, and I will forever be thankful for that.

Taking medication wasn't something I sought out or planned to do. It is something that I have grown used to. It is something that is part of my routine. Taking medications isn't something to frown upon or look down on. We don't make fun of someone who takes care of their broken arm, so I'm not sure why we continue to downplay people getting help for their broken brains. It's something that can is treatable and can be helped with modern medications.

TUMOR

Yes, I have a tumor. It's in the left frontal lobe of my brain, directly behind my eye. Sometimes it causes dull headaches. Other times I don't feel anything at all. But my lifestyle, and even my medications, have all been affected. It's called a cavernoma malformation.

For instance, I'm not supposed to take any type of stimulant (without the a-okay from my neurologist) because it could increase my blood pressure, which causes the cavernoma malformation to act up. (I'm not getting into the specifics of what this is, or it'll turn into a science textbook, and you've read in another chapter science is not my strong suit.)

On a Tuesday, December 8th of 2020, I went to have an MRI, as you know, to rule out MS. I wasn't expecting them to find a tumor; I was just expecting them to tell me whether I had MS or not. I was expecting answers as to why I had certain symptoms. I also wasn't expecting to hear back for a week or so, like they said. Much to my surprise, and horror, I got a call at approximately 5:05pm from my primary care physician saying that she had good news and bad news.

The good news? I didn't have MS, like we were looking for.

The bad news? She found the cavernoma malformation. She immediately scheduled me to meet with a neurosurgeon to begin the stages of what that meant for me. Was I to have surgery? Was it big? What did it affect in my brain? These questions and so many more were rolling around in my brain (ironically enough), but I had to wait two weeks, until January 4th, 2021, to speak to my neurosurgeon.

December 10th, 2021 was also a major day for me. My primary care physician asked the prior Tuesday if I smoked. When I said yes, she explained not only the obvious health risks, but also the risks for my tumor. Smoking could cause it to expand. On Thursday, December 10th, I had my last cigarette. After years and years of smoking (or vaping) I quit cold turkey. It scared me. I did not want to risk my overall health for a cigarette. It took a tumor to quit. It has been one of the best decisions I have ever made.

At the time, I had just moved into my sister and brother-in-law's house. It was during COVID, so the renting/housing market was impossible. We began talking about the possibilities if I had to have surgery. My room was upstairs, so naturally we discussed a makeshift room in the spare room downstairs. We discussed who would take care of me as they both worked.

I was also in the home stretch, as in the final five months, of my undergraduate degree. Would I need to pause school? I was on winter break, and classes would begin again right around the same time I would speak to my neurosurgeon, so life was kind of put on pause for two weeks. It was a lot of planning. I got in touch with my college advisor and began preparing for extra time to complete assignments for worst case scenarios. I began to make decisions based on the what ifs. And I had very little information regarding my tumor—just that I had one, what it was called, and where it was located.

January 4th, 2021 finally rolled around. I remember being on hold for what seemed like an eternity. With my phone on speaker laying on my bed, my sister and I sat motionless waiting for my neurosurgeon to join the call. It took forever. Time truly stood still waiting for that conversation. Finally, she joined the call.

For me, luckily, she said not only was my tumor benign, but that it was small enough that I didn't have to worry about surgery. I still had to have an MRI/MRA done every year, and then bi-yearly to ensure no growth was happening.

I'm happy to report as I type this, I'm on year two and have just started going bi-yearly to have my check-ups done for this tumor. I no longer smoke (over two years free by the time this publishes) and I'm the healthiest I've ever been. I've gained weight, probably due to COVID and medications, but I'm still healthy. In the grand scheme of things, I'm also the happiest I've ever been, too.

I'm a new type of healthy. My mental well-being is being taken care of. That's a different type of peace. When we talk about being healthy, most of us automatically go to gym rats always in the gym and eating nothing fun. What I'm talking about is I'm at peace with how I look and feel.

This tumor taught me that I can't spend life on the side-lines of my own life.

It taught me that I need to be proactive in taking care of myself.

It has taught me to stop taking my health for granted.

It's taught me to listen to my body and speak up for myself.

I found this tumor because I was discussing symptoms of

my mental health. Taking care of my mental well-being put me directly on the path of finding this tumor, and I will forever be thankful for that. So, if you're looking for a sign to take care of your mental health? This is it. Mental health is just as important as your annual check-ups. Your health is a top priority and only you can vouch for yourself. Only you can speak for yourself. Be vocal.

You are your only advocate in this lifetime. You are the only person that is going to know your own body inside and out. Speak up for it. Make sure you're being heard. If you aren't, find another doctor.

Your mental health matters.

ANNOYING THINGS HETERO PEOPLE DO

THINGS our heterosexual counterparts do that we wish they would stop doing. A thread:

- Calling us their "gay friend" (insert lesbian, trans, etc.) rather than just their friend (or sibling, daughter, etc.)
- Gender reveal parties
- Asking us "when we knew" we were queer
- Ask us about gender roles (who pays on the first date, who's the "man" or "woman" in the relationship)
- Assume we have a crush on them
- Ask us questions about sex toys (Do you ask your straight friends about this? Seriously, knock it off.)
- Think all butch/dyke lesbians are into cars
- Attempt threesomes
- Saying "It must be so much easier dating women."
- Project heterosexual gender stereotypes on us
- Jokes about becoming a lesbian "because men are hard"

- Attempt to change our minds
- Assume gay men are ultra-feminine and act a certain way
- Assume bisexual is a phase or a placeholder until you either "go gay or straight"
- Trying to set us up with your other queer friend (also stop asking if we know each other. We don't.)
- Question or doubt our identity
- "Coming out" happens over and over and over again (doctors' offices, new jobs, schools, families, etc.) not just once. Stop asking for our "story"
- Men saying two women are "hot" but being disgusted by two men being together
- Bi/pan erasure in straight passing relationships
- Asking "How did you not know?"
- Saying "I *knew* you were"
- Fetishizing women being together
- Asking if we're attracted to you when you find out we're queer
- Erasing asexuality and their validity
- Assuming demisexual means monogamous
- Asking who the biological parent is
- Asking how the kids were conceived

ALISHA

By now, I know most of you want this chapter. After all, it is an important one. My very own meet-cute. It's definitely my favorite. But I'm just going to forewarn you, you may not like some parts. And that's okay. Some parts we aren't proud of, either, but to keep this as transparent as possible, the truth must be told, and in doing so, we may upset a few people.

Confused? Don't worry, I'll start from the beginning.

But just so you know, I'm currently writing this chapter from our home, in our bed, while my love gently sleeps beside me. And no amount of grief we get will take away the love we share. This I know to be true.

Onward.

We met on Bookstagram, as I stated earlier. She slid into my DM's quicker than it takes you to read this sentence. I say that with a smile on my face, like I know is on yours right now. I always say that, and she always makes fun of me, but it's true. She started the conversation, and that's one conversation I'll forever be thankful for. Before we get to this though, let me back up a little.

I created my Bookstagram the first week of May in 2020, the year the world shut down. Her, the end of October of the same year. We didn't know each other back then. We were simply two nerds creating book accounts, half away across the country from one another, because we knew our friends and families were tired of seeing us post books on our personal pages. Unbeknownst to us, our worlds would collide a little more than two years later.

Her, in a heterosexual marriage with three beautiful children, living in Wisconsin. Me, a single (and self-described and identified then) non-binary individual, living in North Carolina. How our worlds collided, though, would eventually shape our future together. Again, we just didn't know it yet.

As you will see, things get complicated. Messy. Love, rarely, is never as it appears in the movies, tied together neatly with a bow. It's complicated. It has intricacies that few know how to navigate successfully. There are too many feelings involved.

It just gets messy, friends.

You see, it took a Coming Out Story on my end, and a "People You May Know" on her end, for us to find one another, but it happened. As it was bound to. It also took one singular meme posted to a Bookstagram story for our first words to be uttered to one another. But just so the record shows, she followed me first. So technically, she started it. You're welcome.

June 18, 2021.

I posted a funny meme in my Bookstagram stories that said something along the lines of, "Before Pride Month ends, does anybody wanna admit they got a crush on me?" Alisha responded with nothing but a Schitt's Creek David gif that had the words, "Yeah. Hi?" on it with his hand raised. And that my friends, is how our meet cute story began.

With a meme and a gif; a hope and a prayer.

A single comment... that wasn't technically a comment at all.

We flirted for weeks. And by we, I mean she flirted for weeks. Because I was oblivious. Truly, utterly, oblivious. We hit it off with the first messages sent back and forth, though. She made me laugh from the very beginning, as she no doubt has also made you all laugh that know her, too. We talked books, kids, running away from life and all things Bookstagram. It was such an easy conversation to have. Nothing was forced. There was just one problem, though... She was married.

*She was **still** married.*

Navigating this was something we did not take lightly. She felt trapped in a marriage that had run its course, through various happenstances that left her essentially without a dollar to her name. She was trapped. Had no money since she was a stay-at-home parent, had nothing to her name. This is how most toxic relationships begin, and sadly, only get worse from there.

But the connection we had was something fierce. When I say we hit it off, we truly talked non-stop every day. And we have, except for a three-hour window when we got caught by her husband for the first time, when we tried to end it, on my birthday in 2021.

We lasted three hours.

We've been together in some sense, ever since then. Talking non-stop, be it facetime, text messages, or Bookstagram messages, ever since June 18, 2021, and I would not change a single thing.

I know you're thinking less of us, but I did forewarn you. Some parts of our story wouldn't be pretty. In fact, how we started was downright messy, but it's our story and this is how it goes.

As I said, we kept talking, and the more we talked, the more we both questioned what we were to one another. I was questioning why I was hung up on someone who was married and living half a country away from me. Her? She was questioning her sexuality. Her marriage. Her life up until that point. She would question it right up until the first time we had sex.

She questioned it, to some level, until the minute I arrived on our doorstep.

Despite signing a lease together, she still had her reservations…

But I'm getting ahead of myself.

Every chance we got, we talked. I was completely enamored, as was she. We exchanged the "love your face" before we got the nerve to tell each other "I'm in love with you." This went on for a few weeks. Fun fact: she uttered those words first. Even before an "I love you." And we exchanged them just a month, if that, after we began talking. It's always been said that when you know, you know, and we both just *knew*.

Even if the circumstances weren't ideal.

We just connected. And we couldn't get enough of each other. We built a friendship. We built a relationship, without the physical aspect, for six months. We did the long-distance thing. We made it work.

When we were on our infamous three-hour break, I remember her asking me beforehand if there was a chance I'd ever move to Wisconsin, and I replied, "I never say never." At the time, I was doubtful. I had a life in North Carolina, even if I didn't like it. I truly didn't think I'd ever pack up my entire life and move halfway across the country, but I never told her that. Instead, I replied with that line. Because I truly don't ever say never... and this is why: because here I am, a year later, living my best life with the love of my life.

I can't imagine where I would be if we stopped talking for real that day. I know I cried for that three-hour period. I'm sure it was a combination of it being my birthday and it being semi-ruined and the fact that we were no longer talking. It was the longest three hours of my life, and not just because my birthday was ruined. And for anyone doing the math, we started talking June 18, and my birthday is June 24. I felt that way in a six-day period.

When you know, you know, and I knew.

I knew she was something special. I knew she was *it*. She was *the one*. Even if my mind needed time to catch up, my heart already knew. And so did hers.

As many of you know, I'm an avid football fan. Not just any football, Green Bay Packers football. I will eat, sleep and breathe Packers football. I am, as they say, a self-proclaimed cheesehead, and I love it. So, booking a flight to Green Bay, Wisconsin for November of that year, to my family, who didn't know about Alisha (sans my sister) was nothing out of the ordinary. I wanted to be in Titletown. A check off the bucket-list. Easy peasy. I booked a three-night stay. Wednesday night through Saturday morning. We devised a plan. All was set. She would tell her husband she was going to the bookstore and would come see me that Wednesday night instead. And then come and see me Thursday and Friday while the kids were at school.

Except my flight in on Wednesday night was delayed, which meant I couldn't see her as planned. We had to wait until Thursday morning when she dropped off the kids at school. The anticipation was out of this world. We both went to bed that night full of not only disappointment we had to wait another day, but excitement for it at the same time.

I remember what she was wearing when I first laid eyes on her, though. Black leggings, a blue jean button up shirt and her puffy green jacket because it was freezing outside. She brought me McDonald's breakfast and a caramel coffee. I didn't eat it. Barely touched my coffee. There was just *her*.

This is the part where she wants me to go in great detail about our hotel sex, and since I'm a super private person, I won't. But I will say I've never been with someone I was so sure I wanted to spend the rest of my life with. The physical connection matched the emotional one. Sparks, rainbows, unicorn farts and all that jazz. I wanted to stay in that bed forever with her. I did, as events would play out, get to spend the next forty-eight hours with her. Why, you ask? Because her nosey neighbor called her husband and said her dad was at the house, rather than her, with their youngest.

We were caught for the second time.

This time, it was different. The tides had shifted. She was leaving him. For me.

That was petrifying. She was scared. I was scared. But we both knew that being together felt like the surest thing we've ever done. We knew five months in that we were doing this. We knew right then, before then even, that we belonged together. Being together physically just sealed the deal in a sense. Being together physically was everything we thought it would be and more.

She became homeless after that initial hotel visit. She had nowhere to go. She was able to go to the house and grab a child's size suitcase full of clothes and items, but beyond that, she had nowhere to go. She stayed with me and cried in my arms for the next two days. We stayed in that bed. We didn't know what we were doing, we just knew we were meant to be together, and this was the beginning of it actually happening.

It was terrifying and exhilarating.

We had no idea how our story would unfold, just that, right then, in those moments, life was still. Calm.

Finally.

I had to leave that Saturday morning. Incredibly early. So, she stayed until check out. She had no money, nothing to her name but the vehicle she was driving and the child's sized suitcase of belongings. All I had in cash was $67. I left it for her, so she had money to get food or gas or whatever she needed. We've joked about that since then. That all she was good for was $67, and that I should have been Richard Gere in Pretty Woman. I will never live that down. Ever. She tells me all the time she's only worth $67 since that's what I left for her that morning.

Alisha eventually moved into her friend's house for four months. Where she slept on a twin sized mattress on the living room floor. Life was not ideal for her. She barely saw the kids; she had no job because she had been enrolled in school and a stay-at-home parent. She had nothing. To say this was the lowest point in her life would probably be an understatement.

She also finally felt free. She finally felt like she was able to fully be herself. Coming out meant she didn't have to hide who she was anymore. Yes, her marriage had ended. Yes, she was homeless. But she was true to herself, for once, she was doing what she needed to do for herself. For her kids. She needed to be authentically herself, so her kids knew what that looked like. Being yourself is never easy. Life gets in the way. It's hard. It's complicated. It's also messy.

I went home that week with a new perspective on life. I watched the woman I was in love with sacrifice her entire life to be herself. Literally, her entire life. She had nothing. It was liberating. It was also scary for me. No, she wasn't doing it for me. She did it for herself, but I was there. I was the one she wanted to be with.

I was the one.

Now it was all about making sure I made it back to Wisconsin to be there with her. That was the beginning of that, "Oh shit, this is happening" moment for me. That's when it became real. In the back of my mind, I always wondered if I was enough. If I was going to be the one to spend my life with her. I wondered if I would be the one for her.

I was in school for my undergraduate degree at the time and was slated to graduate the following May. I knew I couldn't manage to pack, move and still maintain courses, so moving would have to wait until in between graduation and starting my graduate degree the following year, in 2022. It was hard spending three days together and then going back to not knowing when we were going to see one another. It was debilitating if I'm being one hundred percent honest.

We began talking even more after she was staying with her friend. Our communication shifted from the "I miss you" to "When will I see you again?"

It didn't take long for me to schedule another trip in March of the following year to see her again. This time? For a week.

In between these two visits, a lot changed. She landed a job; we began looking for houses. It was getting more clear that I would be moving halfway across the country for someone. It was exciting and also very scary. I had moved only twice out of state, once a few hours away from home to Virginia, and the other during the military to Missouri. I had never been away from my family for longer than a few months at a time. This was all going to be new to me.

And yet, this is still what I wanted. I knew without a shadow of a doubt that this was the life I wanted, and I wanted to spend it with her.

That week of March truly sped by. She let me be a tourist and took me to the Packers Hall of Fame and all the local spots to eat. We went book shopping at the local Barnes & Noble. We took all the pictures together. I had cheese curds. Most importantly, though? I got to meet the kids for the first time *and* we got the keys to our first rental house.

Meeting the kids was nerve racking to me. I so desperately wanted them to like me but didn't want to come across as over-exuberant to them. I tried to play it cool, but I did wind up playing hide and seek with the five-year-old for hours. So, I call that a win.

They were so open and receptive and by the end of the day, we were all talking and laughing and playing. They're amazing kids.

When she picked me up from the airport, our first stop was to the house so I could see it. She would be moving in the week that I was there. Looking at the house, as empty as it was, felt much like our relationship starting out. We had nothing but each other. It was humbling walking through this house and imagining and talking about all the possibilities that could happen here. We were home. And it felt like it. (And maybe we also had sex upstairs, which she, again, wants me to give details, of which I absolutely will not.)

I moved to Wisconsin on the 10th of May 2022. Daniel, my brother, helped me pack everything up on the 9th. We packed up the entirety of my storage unit and the rest of my belongings at my sister's house and then went back to my stepmom's house to park the U-Haul, eat dinner, and crash. Yes, there's a lesbian joke in there somewhere about U-Hauls. I've said them.

Anyway. We barely slept. We woke up, after barely sleeping from the excitement, around 1:30 in the morning. This trip was going to take us roughly eighteen and a half hours to complete. We had already gotten some drinks and snacks and filled up on gas for the trip earlier the previous day, so we were ready to go when we woke up.

I remember what I was wearing. Grey and white striped ADIDAS shorts with a *To Write Love on Her Arms* long sleeve T-shirt, with my black *Drink Water. Love Hard. Fight Racism.* ballcap on. I can close my eyes and see us stretched out on the bedroom floor before we left. I was a nervous wreck. It was really happening. And the only thought I had was that I wished I could have given my dad, sleeping peacefully in the next room, a hug before I left.

Our ride here was uneventful. We made impeccable time. Stopping through various states along the way for potty breaks or gas fill-ups. We finally got to the house around 3:30 p.m. CST. She was still working but left my copy of the key in the mailbox. I walked into the sweetest love note. Daniel and I just hung out until she got home. We drank, because after an eighteen-and-a-half-hour drive, we wanted some alcohol.

When she got home, we all changed and met her best friend at a local place and had dinner just the four of us. It was the best "welcome home" dinner I've had to date. And if you know anything about me, you know I save receipts of meaningful occasions. It, along with the pictures we took that night, made it into our photo album of our first year together.

Out of all the stories I've read thus far, though, ours is my favorite.

We've done life together since then. The mundane, normal, routine stuff you do with a partner when you live together. There's nothing out of the ordinary that we did.

We just did life.

Until one day I decided I wanted to do life a little differently. Until one day I decided that I was tired of having her as a girlfriend and wanted more. I wanted more out of our lives together. I wanted permanent. Because, like I said at the beginning of this chapter, when you know, you know.

On a Tuesday, September 6, 2022, I proposed. It wasn't out of the movies. It wasn't glamorous. It probably, to most, wasn't even romantic. It was what I thought was best since we had the kids. It was what I thought to be soaked in our many "firsts." I picked the place we had our first home meal together. I picked a spot we gather as a family. I chose a spot that exuded our familial bonds and where we most often are. I chose the living room of our first home.

Before we had furniture, before we had moved in, while we only had the keys, we had our very first meal together on the living room floor. It was Arby's. It wasn't glamorous. It was our first. And it was perfect. I wanted to make memories, just the two of us, in our new home. And so that's the spot I chose.

Since we had the kids (they were at school) that week, I chose to do it on her lunch break from work. She always comes home for lunch. She works maybe five minutes away. Before we get to the nitty gritty of the story you so desperately want to hear though, let me back up a bit…

I ordered the ring on a Thursday morning, September 1st. You got that right, you mathematicians; I waited a whole five days before I proposed. Keeping secrets is hard for me.

Keeping secrets is even harder when you're dating your best friend; I tell Alisha everything.

And I mean everything.

When you tell me a secret, Alisha doesn't count in the "I won't tell anybody." We're a packaged deal. I could not imagine *not* telling her something.

I waited five whole damn days before I popped the question, but before that even happened (I know, you just want the story, this is part of it, too) I had to literally tell everyone, because I CANNOT KEEP SECRETS! Like, the whole world practically knew except Alisha. Her best friends, mine, my self-proclaimed anchovies you met earlier, her dad, my parents… everyone. Everyone knew. I could *not* keep my mouth shut. I was so excited and nervous. I told everyone I felt like I was going to throw-up, and while I didn't, the feeling was very much there. I felt nervous and anxious, and I already have unmedicated, diagnosed inattentive ADHD so it only made matters worse for me.

I couldn't sit still.

I paced.

I bounced off the walls.

I was just mentally ready to be engaged to her.

For an entire week I felt like I was lying to Alisha. It was *the* longest week of my liiiiiife. I had ordered the ring, so it wasn't on my person until, you guessed it, Tuesday, September 6th. I waited approximately six hours to propose once I had the ring in my possession.

That's how much of bad liar I am. In fact, as soon as she walked through the door, she knew something was up. I couldn't help it. I was nervous and anxious! Don't give me the side eye. I can't lie as it is, but to that degree? Forget it. I was done for. There was no way I was withholding that big of news from her for an extended period of time.

Naturally, though, she didn't get to come home at the time she normally does, so it was prolonged by about forty minutes. *I paced.* I was texting everyone until I saw her pull into the driveway. When that happened, I froze and jumped into action simultaneously. My heart was no doubt beating like I just finished a marathon. I placed my phone in the time-lapse camera mode and set it up on our bookshelf facing our sofa. *Still pacing.* Probably had a goofy look on my face. Before she walked in, she could see me bent down holding the ring in front of the camera and smiling this goofy smile.

It wasn't a matter of her saying no, it was all just a matter of how I was going to do it. The buildup. The crescendo. Mostly, I was psyching myself out, like my best friend had already told me. Beyond that, I was just plain ol' scared. So, when you people talk about your significant others proposing, just know their stomachs were in their throats and they probably felt like they were going to pass out from nerves alone— regardless of if you were going to say yes or not.

As I was saying earlier, I sat the phone up on the bookshelf in the living room and started recording it. We were standing in the kitchen while she was making lunch, oblivious to what was about to happen as soon as she sat down in the living room. I stood there and talked to her a bit, still nervous as ever and she knew it. She called me out, but I played it off that it was just my unmedicated ADHD kicking in because I was so jittery.

I went into the living room first and sat down facing the camera. She came in a minute or so behind me and sat down opposite me. We talked for a second and then I dropped to one knee, and said something along the lines of, "I love you. Will you marry me?" in between her freaking out and saying "oh, my god!" The rest was incoherent mumbling.

To say she was surprised was an understatement. We're at

the building stage of our lives right now, so we're tight on money. She never thought in a million years I'd propose this soon. We just didn't have the extra money. Except I'm a sneaky little fucker and I do a thing called what I want. (Not really, just in this scenario. Let me have it.)

To say she wanted to go back to work was an understatement. Her lunch break was the quickest lunch break to date. But she went back, and I was left to play the time-lapse video over and over again.

Telling the kids was fun, though. I teamed up with a friend we have and brainstormed an idea to involve the youngest kid. She was going to send me some play rings so I could give her one, too. We sat the oldest and youngest down and we talked to them about what marriage was and that Mom and I were getting married. I asked them if that was okay. I asked them if it was okay that I married their mom. Their relationships with me matter just as much as my relationship with Alisha. I wanted them to be okay with this decision. Then I told the youngest I had a ring for her like mom had and put it on her finger.

The oldest jokingly immediately asked if he could call me Dad. (I said I didn't care what he called me because I sincerely don't. It's the relationship that matters to me.) His follow-up question was if this meant that we were going to have a baby, of which we promptly shot down. All jokes aside, it went extremely well. They both were ecstatic and bouncing off the walls. It was all I could dream of with them. Even though I was just as scared to talk to them as I was to propose to Alisha.

Our story is still unfolding since I've moved here. Since I've come home. We're still writing this chapter. This chapter will forever be my favorite. No matter how inexplicably messy it may have started out. It wound up beautifully and I'm thankful for every second of it.

As I'm writing this, we've picked the date for the wedding; it'll be in the fall of 2023. That's all I'm going to give you. It will be perfect because it will be ours.

And our story is my favorite story.

KIDS

IF I'M BEING honest with myself, I've always wanted to have kids. Not *me* actually *having* them, but I wanted a family. And if I did, I knew wanted to adopt—or so I thought. Once I reached my thirties, I chalked it up to not having any at all, that it wasn't in the cards.

I had been single for about five years, and I was at peace with that outcome. And before you start quoting how I can be a single parent, adopt by myself, et cetera, that costs *a lot* of money, and also, living in the South, I can be turned away more times than not by adoption agencies. I lack the privilege of being heterosexual *and* married *and* having a high income to afford the adoption. And that's okay (no, it isn't) but that's just how it was for me.

(We seriously need to work on the adoption process. And hello, can we also talk about this economy and the cost of living? Phew.)

I love kids and I desperately wanted them in my life, but to the outside world, it was just another *thing* to me. Something that no one knew I secretly, and oh-so-badly wanted. I had resigned to being the cool adult who swooped in and got to play and do all the fun things and then leave again. That was my role. And damn it, I was going to excel at it.

You kind of give up on certain aspects of your life at times, but secretly still hope they happen, you know? That was kids for me. You want things so badly, but you don't want to say them out loud for fear of them not coming true and having everyone feel sorry for you instead.

That's how I felt for a long time.

I saw so many friends, both hetero and homosexual, settling down and having families and there I was: solo. Or at least having short-term failed relationships one right after another. Something wasn't adding up. I tried and failed and tried and failed so many times I simply decided to stay single. It was a conscious choice.

You make plans for yourself only for life to laugh directly in your face, though. Because while I was too busy accepting my child-less fate, life was busy ensuring my life would be fulfilled in every single way possible... including three bonus kids whom I have in my life now.

And I'm lucky. I have these amazing kids that add so much joy to my life for three totally separate reasons.

I met Alisha, fell in love and managed to get the package deal. Everything I had ever dreamed of all rolled into one. It is a dream come true. But don't let me fool you, now there's a parent's role in play. And let me tell you, stay-at-home parenting is a Poopalooza. A shitpocalypse. A shitnado.

Things get messy.

Like this one time, the youngest shit her swimsuit. Outside. All over the wall, the door, herself. This continued into the house. You see, I heard her come in, but hadn't heard anything from her in a few minutes and that's highly unlike her. It was quiet. *Eerily* quiet. *Too* quiet. If you have kids, you know: when they're quiet, that's when chaos ensues.

This was my first lesson.

I found this tiny tot, much to my dismay and hers, in the bathroom. Coated in her own shit. She had it everywhere. In the sink, the trashcan, down her leg, and *actual* turds in her hands. Y'all, there was shit *everywhere*. I was both horrified and impressed by how much shit there was in a matter of minutes.

Naturally, because I'm a semi-normal functioning adult, I gag when I smell putrid smells such as vomit or shit of that nature. I had to *gently* push this child out my line of sight to the toilet to throw-up.

With all of this chaos around me.

When the girl child and I locked eyes, I'm truly *still* unsure who was more mortified: me, the 'adult' who was supposed to be in charge, or her, the turd in question. All I knew to do was again, *gently*, toss her into the shower. I recall her pleading for a bath. But there was shit all over her. Bath? Forget it.

While she was in the shower, I had to clean up the shit-storm in the bathroom. I wound up with it in my socks (some-how) and permanently engrained in my sandals so much that I wound up throwing them away. It was down the hallway on the floor. There was a literal trail of shit from outside to inside.

While she was in the shower finding the true color of her skin, I called Alisha freaking out. I had a huge dilemma. Do I clean out her swimsuit of shit and risk throwing up again or was it safe to throw it all in the washing machine and throw a hail Mary that it would all get clean?

When she answered I began sputtering about shit every-where. I was met with laughter. Pure, unadulterated laughter. The kicker? She only had like ten minutes left of work before she was home. This child waited until her mom was *almost* done with work to have the biggest shit in her life, *in her swimsuit*. Outside. The only question that kept recurring in my mind was, "She couldn't have waited until her mom got home to do this?"

When Alisha assured me that I could, in fact, throw a hail mary and toss all the clothes in the washing machine, I was relieved. I finally had the bathroom and the child cleaned, and *then* Alisha came home.

She was pissed.

There was shit all over the door outside. Not just the door, the handle, too. The wall beside the door. There were turds outside on the pavement where the girl child had tried to dig it out of her swimsuit and hide it. It was a mess. A huge, shitty mess. We actually just recently found the spot in which it started outside. Again, shit on the walls.

This story sums up this kid perfectly. She's a force to be reckoned with. She'll look you dead in the face, tell you no, but then immediately after, tell you she loves you to the moon and back times infinity with the hugest hug you'll ever get. She's fierce. She's sweet and she knows exactly what she's going to do. Underneath that tough exterior, she's a cuddle bug. She will, "Cole" and Bluey me to death one day. But she's going to be a world changer, that one.

This was my first lesson in Parenting 101—within just two months of being here. I had formally been inducted into bonus parent land. Whatever that means, I had arrived in all its glory.

I tell you that story to make you laugh at me (or with me), but also to remind you that I got what I asked for. To have kids. And that's messy. Having kids is messy. My life was never messy before them. I was single. My money went to whatever I wanted it to go to, whenever I wanted. I was self-ish. Meaning I was concerned only with myself—the perks of being single. I dated myself often and frequently and did whatever I wanted when I wanted. And that's perfectly okay. I was single, after all.

How quickly that changed when I started dating Alisha and she moved into our new home. We had to start over with nothing. No toys. No clothes. Absolutely nothing. We're still trying to play catch up with the kids and what they have. My priorities shifted. Now it's all about them. It's making sure they're going to have the best Christmas. It's making sure they're taken care of right now and my needs go last. It's no longer about what I want when I want. It's about what they want and need at this moment. It's putting them first and foremost. Always.

And then there's the middle kiddo. He's my pal. My buddy. He's the sweetest boy you'll ever meet – cuddly, confident and knows exactly what he wants and when he wants it. He's taught me more about life than anyone else has thus far, and this kid is seven.

He's taught me how to navigate this world. And by navigate, I mean that he's taught me that my life is my own and I don't need to worry about what anyone else thinks, says, or does. He's taught me that living life is on my terms, and mine only. He teaches me every day that words matter. Not because they get repeated by smaller ears, but because that's how others see themselves: through the words you say to them.

My words matter because his mental health is important. I now use them wisely. I choose my words very carefully. I always tell him, "Easy," when he gets carried away or jumps around on the furniture. He repeats that now when he knows he's being a little too rough. My words matter. Especially knowing whatever I say, he takes to heart. My words echo into the depths of his brilliant little mind and then come out randomly because he recites things.

This kid has taught me that life goes only at one speed: mine. It goes at the speed I'm most comfortable with. It doesn't stop, slow down, or move faster just because someone else is doing it that way. It goes my speed at all times, and that speed is perfect.

He's taught me to slow the fuck down.

It allows me to enjoy the little things. It allows me to enjoy the small moments. It means I'm open and receptive to new ideas and thoughts around me. It means I'm not following anyone's lead and I'm taking life at my own pace. I am my own leader. I walk to the beat of my own drum. He's taught me to do something only when I'm ready. Everyone else can wait; my time will come only when I decide. This kid is magic.

He's taught me that showing love takes on so many different forms. Not just the well-known, "I love you," but in random hugs, and "I've missed you's," and smiles and always the random times when he runs and crashes into you and just stays there with his arms wrapped around you. It doesn't show up the way neurotypical people are used to. You don't have to "look for it." His love is loud. Louder than any love I've ever experienced. His love is fierce. Because it's genuine. It's pure and cathartic and intense. It's also soft and caring and natural. He makes no qualms about loving someone or showing those around him affection. If he doesn't want to hug you, he isn't going to. And that's the way it should be.

I've learned from him that flappy equals happy. That puzzle pieces and the color blue and Autism Speaks is a sham and distasteful. I've learned that the infinity symbol and the color red are the way to go. I've learned that neurotypical people don't hold enough space or grace for neurodivergent people. That regardless of whether they choose to or not, they do not make a world that's accessible for everyone. That they let people fall through the cracks and treat them as an afterthought.

You see, he has autism. He's on the spectrum. His magical little brain is lightyears ahead of us, and we will never catch up to how brilliant he is. He tells you what he needs in his own language and it's up to you to understand. Yes, he may be different, but so are the rest of us. Being different makes the world go 'round. I've learned to see the world through the lens of a seven-year-old child who has autism, and it can be tiring. It's always, "Go, go, go" and never "stop and smell the roses." It's always rushing around and never getting so excited about the little things you just can't contain your excitement.

This is where the flappy equals happy comes into play. His little arms flap up and down when he's happy and he jumps up and down and it's the single most adorable thing I've ever seen. He expresses his happiness in ways that are liberating and celebratory. He doesn't shy away from showing his exact emotions at any given time.

What a way to live life.

Not hiding your emotions.

All of this a seven-year-old has taught me, and as I'm writing this, I've spent three months learning from him. I can't imagine the lessons he's going to teach me down the road. I still have a lot to learn, but that boy will change the world, too.

But then there's the oldest boy. Talk about smart. He can tell you anything about everything with just one simple question. He'll, "Hey, guess what!" you to death, but the facts that spew from that brilliant little mind? Blows my big mind to shreds.

He's obsessed with Pokémon and Mario and playing

video games like any other prepubescent little boy, but also, he stays watching educational videos on YouTube. He's a stickler for rules and following them and also ensuring his siblings follow them, too. He's nine years old and will still hold my hand crossing the street to school. He will be the one to grab it, and every time he does, he grabs at my heart right along with it.

He's such a smart little boy. He's always the last one up in the mornings (which isn't late, we're talking 7:30 a.m.) and will come crawl into our bed and snuggle and giggle until it's time we all get up. His feelings get hurt easily, so again, watching my words and tone is super important. He is as tender hearted as they come, and I am so enamored with that boy. He's going to grow up and change the world with the most tender heart I know.

These kids have given my life a new sense of purpose. They've created new reasons to live and ensure I'm living my best life so they can witness what that looks like. They've made sure I am always true to myself because I want them to know what that looks like. They make sure I'm loving their mom out loud in ways that are gentle and fierce and healthy, so they know what true love looks like inside and outside. I want them to know what a healthy relationship and friendship looks like, and that means forever dating their mom. Spoiling her with the little things in front of them. Speaking words of affirmation to her. Being affectionate.

These kids have taught me patience. For so long I have been by myself. So, it was always when I wanted to do something. Nope. They teach me that they will do things on their own time, and I have to be okay with that. They teach me every day that my time is on their time, and sometimes that's an adjustment. I'm not always good at being patient. This is usually when one of them will barricade me with a huge hug. Their internal little clocks just *know*.

I'm still learning. There truly is no bonus parent booklet that you can read to learn to navigate helping raise kids. There's no book to teach you how to effectively co-parent. This shit takes time and effort and tears and blood and sweat —okay, maybe not the last two, but it does cause heartache. It's wanting what's best for these kids but not knowing how to do it, trying not to fuck it up, and trying to make sure you're doing everything to the best of your ability.

That's fucking hard.

And draining.

I also have mental health issues and generalized anxiety disorder. Loud noises overwhelm me. More than one thing going on at a time overwhelms me. Can you see where I'm going with this? It's nothing for the television and a tablet to be going full speed while another tries to talk over them both, all while invading your personal space. It's *a lot*. Alisha knows this, so it's nothing for me to say, "Hey, I need a time out," and go to our bedroom to decompress for a little bit. Be it mindlessly scroll or read for a little while. She can see it sometimes before I can verbalize it and will beat me to it by telling me to get lost for a few minutes.

There's no quick fix for the combination of mental health and kids. It's like you're conditioned to be this perfect parent who has their shit together that doesn't experience bad days ever, let alone have mental health problems. It's like you're expected to be happy and carefree without breaks and that's bullshit. If I've learned one thing, it's that your own mental well-being is essential to taking care of kids. That in order to properly take care of your kids, you need to prioritize your mental well-being first.

In saying that, I love these kids. I love how they teach me

to check myself or they'll check me *for* me. I couldn't imagine my life without them now. My life is immeasurably better because of them.

While we're on the subject of kids, I'd like to address something. Just because I didn't *have* them, doesn't make me love them any less or any differently. I hate that shit. What if I *couldn't* have kids and adopted instead? Does my love not equate to parents who gave birth? Does my love not measure up to someone who gave birth? Will it never be enough? Will the kids think I love them less because I didn't birth them? No, they won't.

And since they won't, you shouldn't comment on someone who didn't give birth. The reasons are numerous. Some can't have children. Some have tried and failed. And still, there are those like me that choose not to give birth because we *just don't want to*. And all those reasons are valid. These reasons, however, do not take away from the love we have to give.

Key takeaway: do not, under any circumstance, tell someone that they don't know a parent's love because they didn't give birth. That's bullshit. The end.

BONUS PARENTING IS...

Bonus parenting is a unique kind of battle. You're torn between not overstepping and making sure the kids are well-adjusted and like you. You're making sure they're taken care of and letting them know that you will do your best to take care of them in all ways. There are zero manuals.

Being a bonus parent has taught me so much. Here is what I've learned thus far:

- Bonus parenting is rescheduling an important doctor's appointment four times because you don't always have access to adequate childcare. *(But you get extra time with them.)*
- Bonus parenting is losing sleep because they wake up as the ass crack of dawn every morning. *(But they give you cuddles.)*
- Bonus parenting is picking up toys after them all day long. *(But they're able-bodied.)*
- Bonus parenting is hiding in a room because you need a break. *(But the fact they're looking for you means they miss you.)*

- Bonus parenting is hiding your favorite snacks. *(But giving them some anyway.)*
- Bonus parenting is second guessing your every move. *(But knowing you're doing everything you can do right by them.)*
- Bonus parenting is being overstimulated by all the loud noises they make with their electronics. *(But that means they are privileged to have them.)*
- Bonus parenting is letting your food get cold because you're too busy getting them seconds. *(But they're fed and there's food at their disposal.)*
- Bonus parenting is chasing them around to brush their teeth and take their meds. *(But they have access to healthcare.)*
- Bonus parenting is your coffee getting cold because they demand breakfast as soon as they wake up. *(Because they know you are their provider.)*
- Bonus parenting is watching the same cartoon over and over again because the youngest loves it. *(But they're learning new things and have access to a television.)*
- Bonus parenting is them talking your ear off from the time their little eyes open to the time their little heads hit their pillows. *(But they trust you to talk to you about anything.)*
- Bonus parenting is eating a donut and guzzling a fountain soda in the confines of your car in a gas station parking lot (Kwik Trip or bust) to regain composure because you feel like you've done nothing but fail all day before walking back inside. *(But knowing the kids are waiting for you to get home is priceless.)*

Bonus parenting is not a walk in the park, no matter what anyone tries to tell you. It's messy and complicated and throw in co-parenting and you may as well be yelling at a brick wall (and losing) sometimes. But what I do know is that there are three kids that I adore. There are three kids that adore me. And at the end of the day, that's all I carry with me.

All of that love.

But sometimes you just need a reminder that you're doing an awesome job, friends. So, if you're reading this and you need a donut and a fountain soda, here's your sign.

REDECORATING

Isn't an ending a bittersweet thing? No friends, this isn't really the ending, it's only the beginning.

I'm redecorating my space. This time I have help in the form of a partner. A confidant. A best friend.

A soulmate.

That word is so funny. Soulmates can be anyone, a stranger reading your favorite book, friends, lovers, there's no one singular way to define that word. Too often we get caught up in the fact that it *must* mean partner. To me, for this chapter, it does. At least this time. To me, I've found my spark, my light, my person. I've found the one of whom I can be authentically myself. I've found my home.

Sometimes home is a feeling of arriving. It's changing your body to match how you've always felt inside. It's changing your name. It's changing your pronouns. It's coming out. It's staying in. It's leaving that toxic person. It's moving to a different state. It's loving yourself. It's cutting your hair. It's growing it out. It's painting your fingernails. It's waking up earlier than your family to have that hour of alone time and basking in the beautiful sunrise with coffee in hand. It's stopping what you're doing and catching those moments of pure bliss around you and just soaking it in.

Sometimes searching for home looks like a thousand different things. Sometimes searching means getting lost, redirected, and lost again until, before we know it, we find ourselves at our destination. Home will forever be redefined as we continue to evolve into ourselves. And sometimes we get to continuously redecorate our homes with our soulmates.

I'm here, one week into moving eighteen hours away from my family, while my love makes dinner for the kids; the kids watching TV, running amuck, playing on their tablets while I sit here in the corner of the living room soaking it all up.

Dare I say, even inspired.

I was hesitant that with three kids in tow, it would leave little time for writing, but I find myself soaking in the time with them and sneaking away to write when they're watching a movie because it leaves me feeling overwhelmed with love. The hustle and bustle and non-stop activities and movements around me cause me to stop and reflect on so much—like why I chose to pack up my life and move eighteen hours away from my birthplace to a new home. The funny thing is this feels like home. This *is* home.

Being with Alisha is the easiest thing I have ever done in my life.

Don't get me wrong, we still have our disagreements. Some would argue against that saying our relationship is still new so we're in that "honeymoon" phase, but I counter that. Because when a relationship is right, it just ebbs and flows naturally. And that's what we do.

We fit.

We work.

And we work at it together, rather than against, which is what most people fail to understand.

We know we're one another's home base. We communicate. We talk about what's wrong and how to fix it. It's always us versus the problem; never us against one another. We're decorating our home with love and compassion; with mutual respect and understanding. My soulmate is my best friend. I'm home.

Some people have soulmates in many different facets. I'm lucky to be redecorating my home, figuratively and metaphorically, with mine.

And remember we're all just walking each other home. Be kind to one another on our journeys there. We're all coming home.

DEAR TWENTY-YEAR-OLD-ME

THIS WILL BE the year you begin to find, love, and discover yourself. Take your time. You have the rest of your life. You don't have to have all the answers right away. Don't rush. Just be.

This will be the year your family, church family and friends become the cruelest people in your life. Your first bullies will be these people. Don't let this deter you from living authentically. They will steal years of your life if you let them, so don't.

Live in your love. As much as this may hurt you, you *will* make friendships that will last for a decade (and counting). You will begin to create your own family without even knowing. This family will give you all the space you need to be yourself.

This will be the year you will unlearn what was expected of you and begin learning who you really are. Unpack carefully; take your time. You're becoming who you've always been meant to be. This will take time. Allow yourself space to grieve who you were.

This will be the year you experience life being free for the first time. Soak it up. Take it all in. Slow down and enjoy it. You deserve it.

This will be the year of major heartache, tears, pain and oh so many questions. Feel it all and ask them all, but always remember you're only responsible for you. The people who harmed you will answer for their hurtful words and actions, not you.

Put the hurt where it goes.

It was never yours to hold in the first place.

This will be the year your life truly begins. Have fun. Make memories. Build your foundation solid so it can withstand your journey home. It will be difficult for a while, but you're growing. Growing pains hurt sometimes. Don't give up. The peaks are way more beautiful than the valleys.

If I could tell you one thing, 20-Year-Old Me, it's that your life will ebb and flow with heartache and joyous moments. You will come home to yourself over and over again. Trying on new labels, pronouns, and seeing how they fit. Even discovering your name. These things take time and are meant to be experienced, not expected right away.

If I could tell you anything, 20-Year-Old Me, it's that the next fifteen years you will continue to unpack emotions and the pain caused from this year, but you also learn to put those stones thrown where they belong, as a path to helping you live more authentically.

You deserve to take up space in all your many facets.

Please don't shrink yourself for others.

You will continue to evolve as you get older, and that's the natural part of life. Don't become stagnant in one phase because you're scared of the next. Life is meant to be lived, and then learned.

You will continue growing into yourself; let yourself evolve. You were never meant to stay the same.

Your journey is beautiful.

Don't let anyone steal it.

Your love is meant to be celebrated; find people to celebrate it with.

Go to therapy; and stay there.

You're going to do great things with your pain. Work through your grief, sit with it. Learn from it. These tools will help the future version you.

You'll make mistakes; learn from them.

You'll have heartbreaks and bad relationships; continue to love.

You'll make new friends and then lose some. Remember everyone is for a reason, season, or a lifetime. Don't let people overstay their welcome.

You'll have a horrible sense of fashion—cringeworthy, actually, but we won't discuss that part. Ever.

You'll be a shitty person to some and the best to others; apologize and learn accordingly.

You'll discover happiness isn't at the bottom of a bottle, but you'll still have funny stories from that "one time" anyway.

But most importantly, 20-Year-Old Me, you won't feel trapped in a life you don't belong in. You'll replace that anger and disdain with genuine happiness and laughter. You will love who you are even as you are still striving to become a better you.

If I can tell you anything, 20-Year-Old Me, it's that I'm so proud of how far you will go in fifteen years, and I cannot wait to see where you will be in fifteen more. Your story isn't over yet—keep writing it.

Love,

Thirty-Five-Year-Old Me

To you, Alisha
I am coming home to you.
My forever love.

ACKNOWLEDGMENTS

For some reason, I set out to write about the most difficult things in my life and lay myself bare and exposed for the world to see. A normally extremely private person, I just put myself on blast. I hope in between these covers you've found out a little more about yourself. I hope you've reckoned with who you are and who you hope to become. Above all, I hope home is a place you know.

This book wouldn't have been possible without several people. I'll attempt to list them but will probably fall short. Please know I have no intentions of leaving anyone out, but I'll do my best to include everyone who has impacted my life.

My immediate family, whom I love and adore. My mom, my dad, and my kid sister. All who have helped me grow exponentially. My brother and stepmom who have supported me in every step of the way—regardless of if they know it or not.

To Alisha, my biggest cheerleader. The reason this book has a happy ending. The reason I have the life I do. The reason I pinch myself every day thanking the universe for the life and love I have. Without you, my life would certainly not make sense. I love you always and forever and can't wait to see what the future has in store for us.

My anchovies. We've laughed together, celebrated, mourned, and cracked jokes in-between. You all have each enriched my life individually and together as a group. Thank you will never be enough.

To my sib, without you, this book wouldn't have even been possible. You've been my editor, my sounding board, my proof-reader. Above all, you've been one of the biggest cheerleaders. Even reading a memoir when it isn't your cup of coffee. Thank you a million times over. Heart chew. *Monkey emoji.*

To Tressie, my in real life best friend since I was nine. I cannot imagine a life without you and your family in it. You always know exactly what to say when I need to hear it the most. Thank you for always believing in me. For giving me the space to be myself. I love you more than anything.

To the traditionally published authors who blurbed my book, Addie, Alicia, and Courtney. Your words meant everything to me. The time you took to give my book a chance meant the world. Thank you for giving an indie author a chance to shine and feel seen. Thank you for the friendships created, the feedback, and the encouragement.

To my beta readers early on. Thank you for believing in my words. Thank you for understanding I am a work in progress just as my book. Thank you for believing in me.

To you, dear reader, thank you, thank you, thank you. For not only buying this book but reading it. For giving an indie author a chance. For giving a trans non-binary person a voice. For listening to that voice.

I will forever be indebted to the educators who taught me, the two mentioned in this book and the ones I failed to write stories about, though I have dozens. Educators are, without a shadow of a doubt, the ones who kept me on track during the worst times of my life as a child, and for that, I will forever be indebted to them.

Thank you will never be enough, and yet I am endlessly thankful for you. With all my love and gratitude,

Sawyer Cole

ABOUT THE AUTHOR

Sawyer Cole is from small town Yadkinville, North Carolina. They currently reside in Green Bay, Wisconsin with their fiancée and three kids. They are currently enrolled in the graduate program at Southern New Hampshire University in the child and adolescent psychology program.

When they aren't wrangling three children, their hobbies include reading, writing, and all things book related. They have been an avid reader since childhood and will continue this into their late adulthood.

They're also an avid football fan: Go Pack Go!

Ingram Content Group UK Ltd.
Milton Keynes UK
UKHW021959220323
418981UK00013B/452